Understanding Addiction and Recovery Through a Child's Eyes

Dear Graham,
    Celebrate the
difference you make.
        Love,

        Terry Mae

Understanding Addiction and Recovery Through a Child's Eyes

Help, Hope, and Healing for the Family

Jerry Moe, M.A., M.A.C., C.E.T. II

Health Communications, Inc.
Deerfield Beach, Florida

www.hcibooks.com

Names have been changed to protect the confidentiality and privacy of individuals.

Library of Congress Cataloging-in-Publication Data

Moe, Jerry.
Understanding addiction and recovery through a child's eyes : hope,
help, and healing for the family / Jerry Moe.
    p. cm.
    Includes index.
    ISBN-13: 978-0-7573-0611-2 (trade paper)
    ISBN-10: 0-7573-0611-X (trade paper)
    1. Children of alcoholics—United States—Psychology.
    2. Children of alcoholics—Mental health—United States.
    3. Children of drug addicts—United States—Psychology.
    4. Children of drug addicts—Mental health—United States.
    5. Stress in children—United States. 6. Self-esteem in children—
United States. I. Title.
    HV5132.M64 2007
    362.29'13—dc22

                                                           2007032437

Publisher: Health Communications, Inc.
            3201 S.W. 15th Street
            Deerfield Beach, FL 33442-8190

Cover design by Andrea Perrine Brower
Interior design and formatting by Lawna Patterson Oldfield

This book of
hope, resilience, and love
is dedicated to Brent and to all
children from addicted families.

Contents

CHAPTER THREE: Simple Lessons

CHAPTER FOUR: The Rock Garden

CHAPTER FIVE: Let the Healing Begin

Games and Activities

Acknowledgments

T his book would never have happened without the love and support of countless family members, colleagues, and friends. Without a doubt, my wife Michelle remains a constant source of inspiration and love. Karen Mayers gently guided me along, even at those times I was ready to give up. Teri Peluso stretched my vision of the book and helped make it so much more than I could ever imagine. Betty LaPorte, Sis Wenger, and Joan Connor Clark offered invaluable comments and suggestions to strengthen and deepen the text. Allison Janse put it together in her kind, loving way.

Over the past many years, I've worked at three treatment centers: Sequoia Hospital Alcohol and Drug Recovery Program, Sierra Tucson, and the Betty Ford Center. While each has a distinct philosophy and unique program offerings, they have all been unwavering in their support of treating alcoholism and other drug addiction as a family disease. All three have provided the resources necessary to establish and build solid children's programs. Thanks for your vision, commitment, and support.

Special kudos to all the incredible facilitators I've been blessed to work with through the years. I'm reluctant to start naming you as I'll invariably leave someone out in the process. You know who you are. You have taught me lots, and it's been an honor to share this special work. It's together that we make a difference.

Children need caring adults to take them to get help. I salute all the grown-ups through the years who've made it a priority to get their children and grandchildren to group. Many are giving these special kids the gift they wished they could have had as children— a safe place to grow, learn, play, trust, and heal. Thanks for your trust, love, and dedication to make life better for your families.

Lastly, I applaud all the children who've come through the various programs over the years. Your courage, strength, and resilience are simply awesome. You have been my best teachers. I think about you and pray for you regularly. I love you. Here's hoping I touched your lives almost as much as you've touched mine. No matter where life takes you and what challenges you face, you are not alone and there are safe people and places to help. Never, ever forget that you are special and loved.

Introduction

I have something very special and magical to share with you in the pages of this book. I have spent my adult life in the company of children who have been my teachers. Our paths did not cross because they were exceptionally smart, had demonstrated unusual abilities, or exhibited character traits that belied their years—although these are definitely all ways in which I would describe "my" kids. Rather we got to know each other because someone in their life was addicted to alcohol or other drugs.

For thirty years I have had a front-row seat in group, watching, learning, and helping these youngest victims of addicted families. They live with a legacy that can break hearts and destroy souls—one they did not choose but was thrust upon them by the adults around them.

These groups have taken place in church basements, community programs, and treatment centers, both large and small. Many of these kids live with active addicts or alcoholics; others are referred because a parent is in treatment. They all arrive carrying secrets and shame. Many feel strange, different, and full of guilt. Some see themselves as helpless, worthless, and bad. Then comes the magic.

They find their voice and express their worries, problems, and feelings, and we help them develop coping skills to help care for themselves and keep themselves safe. These children can and do heal from the adverse impact of family addiction by initiating and deepening the healing process before they reach adolescence. They survive and thrive because of their resilience, intuition, intelligence, honesty, and need to trust and love, traits learned in tandem with others who have had similar experiences.

And what's special and magical? The healing process transcends the children and has a dramatic impact on the entire family system—especially the parents. The love and care these kids feel as they confront their parent's disease often stops adults in their tracks and gives them a new, deeper commitment to breaking the multigenerational legacy of addiction.

One of the most rewarding parts of my work is seeing the frightened, confused child grow into a confident, resilient, capable young adult. If you work with children, you know what I mean. Virtually all adults, especially parents and grandparents, hope for this for all children.

In *Understanding Addiction and Recovery Through a Child's Eyes* I am the children's voice, sharing their experiences and stories to help adults better understand addiction from a kid's perspective. Interlaced among the children's stories are lessons learned, techniques used successfully, and pitfalls to avoid, based on my work as a children's counselor for many years. And, to give the reader a sense of the lasting impact of therapeutic intervention on children, each chapter opens with a glimpse into the life of the same family, sharing their journey from the time they walked in the door for a program to the present. The tools each family member learned in recovery have served them well individually, and as a family, through triumph and tragedy.

Each story will remind you that children have a unique way of viewing the world with innocence, wonder, spontaneity, and awe. *Understanding Addiction and Recovery Through a Child's Eyes* promotes personal growth and long-term recovery for children and their families through simple techniques and tools everyone can use.

Whether you are a parent, grandparent, counselor, teacher, minister, youth worker, guardian, or caregiver—in recovery or not—*Understanding Addiction and Recovery Through a Child's Eyes* has a message I hope you will hear: There is hope for children of all ages who have been hurt by addiction in their families. It is time to recognize the children's pain and allow them to be an integral part of family healing.

CHAPTER ONE

Family Portraits

Only the Beginning

hey walked into the Kids' Zone looking nervous and confused, and a cloud of sadness seemed to hang over them while they settled into their seats in the group room. The father, Brent, was welling up with tears as he scanned the child-friendly environment. Amidst all these bubbling emotions, what stood out clearly was the love they had for each other.

Angela was a beautiful nine-year-old with huge eyes and an expressive face. She held her father's hand gently, yet firmly, and gazed up at him often, smiling when their eyes met. Brendan, a rambunctious six-year-old, excitedly jumped from his chair into his dad's lap many times over the next several minutes and hugged Dad every time he landed on him. Brent kept his kids close and quietly reassured them. Without a doubt, he was very proud of them. This is how it all began.

Brent was struggling with early recovery and had been sober for about four months. He and his wife, Judy, wanted to make things right for their kids. Addiction had wreaked havoc on this family, and it continued to mess with everyone even though the drinking had stopped.

It didn't take long for these kids to feel safe and begin to open up. Within the first hour after Dad left the room for the parent orientation, Angela talked about her parents fighting and how she hated it when they got separated. "Sometimes I felt so sad and scared that I had to come home from school. I couldn't get my work done."

Brendan, taking emotional cues from his sister, gradually let the others into his world. "Why does my dad have to go to all those meetings?" he began. "I want my dad to stay home and play with me," he emphatically told the group. Both kids were fearful, confused, and angry, yet they settled in quickly and were eager for some answers.

A critical part of the first day of the program is helping the kids to differentiate the person they love from the disease that consumes them. We play a powerful game called Addiction to bring this important lesson to life. I role-play Addiction to make this disease concrete so youngsters can see it, watch it, listen to it, react to it, and have feelings about it. If they want to play, one by one the children get to meet Addiction and listen to all the lies: "I'll make all your problems disappear"; "You'll only feel happy and joy with me"; "I'll make you stronger, smarter, and funnier, and give you friends." They can see and feel that this illness sets a huge trap and, if a person goes along, he or she can quickly get hooked. At this point Addiction holds on to the person, and he or she can't get away. This is a powerful image for kids to see.

Brendan and Angela both played the game. Brendan ended up getting trapped and in a playful way got a sense of his dad's struggles. Angela said no to the disease and never got hooked by it. At the end of the activity she sadly remarked, "I wish my dad had said no to addiction a long time ago." Almost all the other kids nodded their heads at her keen insight.

On the second day, when it was time to write their stories, Angela hesitated. When I checked in with her she softly whispered, "I don't want to hurt my dad. He's getting better now."

"I don't want you to hurt your dad either," I explained. "Just tell on his disease."

Angela's eyes grew wide as she put her pencil to the paper and the words flew out. Her story ended up being ten pages long as she poured out her heart and soul. Brendan drew a couple of pictures, as writing was too arduous a task for this little guy. Using only a pencil, he drew his mom and dad fighting, with him standing off to the side crying. His parents both looked angry, and he was clearly so sad. This was a simple yet powerful picture.

It was day three of the program, and Angela went first. She pulled her chair out to the center of the circle and asked her dad to bring his out as well. I am always amazed at the courage and strength children possess. I'm not sure I could have ever done what Angela was about to do when I was nine years old. When I asked father and daughter to look at each other, Angela started to cry. Brent let his daughter know that he really wanted her to tell the truth and promised she wouldn't get in trouble for it.

She began by saying, "Daddy, I love you. I always have and always will. This is about your addiction." Tears streamed down Brent's cheeks, yet his face and body posture were open and reassuring. Angela did an incredible job as she talked about the yelling and fighting. While she carefully edited what she read and what she decided to leave out as she went along, her anger at the disease and love for her father shined through. It was clear; she didn't want to hurt him. When she finished reading, I asked if she wanted to tell her dad anything else. All she said was, "I don't want to lose you, Daddy," before rushing into his arms. They held each other tightly and cried. Judy, who was home with a sick baby, had missed a special moment.

Brendan was brave and honest, too. He showed his drawings and shared his feelings of sadness and confusion. This was extremely difficult for him because he loved his dad so much. He was holding back for lots of reasons: not wanting to hurt Dad, afraid that Dad might get mad, worried that he might get upset and drink again. "Please stay home with us," Brendan told his dad at the end of the sharing. Pain was written all over this little guy's face. Taking another cue from his big sister, his final comments were even more telling. "I hate addiction," he blurted out in a very, very angry tone.

Dad silently nodded his head, reached out to his son, and quietly held him tightly. "Brendan, I hate addiction, too."

Who Are They?

T hey arrive—all different shapes, sizes, and colors—boys and girls like Angela and Brendan, accompanied by at least one adult who deeply cares about them. They anxiously sit around the circle waiting for the festivities to begin. There's such diversity present in the room: nuclear families; single-parent families; divorced, blended, and adopted families; foster families; gay families; racially mixed families; *all* families. Addiction is truly an equal-opportunity disease. Addiction is blind to age, race, gender, culture, level of education, sexual orientation, and socioeconomic status.

Some of these special kids have a parent in recovery; others have a loved one still active in their disease. A lucky few have never seen their parent take a drink or drug because the parent has been in recovery during the child's entire life. Other kids will never see their loved one again—this can be a fatal disease. They may be here for a parent, grandparent, aunt, uncle, or a sibling. Each is so different and yet the same in a single breath.

While they nervously scan the room for any clues as to what's about to unfold, little do these children realize they are finally "home." While they and their families may look so different, each knows firsthand the confusion and pain of living with this insidious illness. Most relate to the sadness, hurt, loneliness, and anger of broken promises, verbal violence, neglect, and family instability.

Many know all too well the stress, constant fear, and nagging worry about losing a loved one forever to drinking or drugs. Many believe somehow it really is all their fault, and despite heroic efforts, they never seem to make things okay. The embarrassment, isolation, silence, and secrecy are often eerily similar. They have often felt so all alone, but now there's a faint glimpse that they're not. Different yet the same. Now the journey begins.

The Alien

Kids enter the children's program in many different ways. Some walk in very nervous and scared about what will transpire. Maybe they worry that someone will tell them that it truly is all their fault. Others breeze in joyfully with huge smiles on their faces. Somehow they sense this is a safe place, and they delight in being with other youngsters dealing with similar problems, feelings, and concerns. Still others are very confused, as the grownups in their lives couldn't find the words to adequately explain what they were doing here.

My most important responsibility that first hour is to help everyone settle into the process. This can be an arduous task as some are guarded, others resistant, some on the verge of tears, and still others acting like good old friends from long ago. We slowly yet methodically weave our way through a number of important tasks in those mood-setting sixty minutes. Group members get to decorate folders to their specific customizations. Each youngster gets to self-address an envelope so we can send them something special once the program ends. (This is a very simple way to assess reading and writing skills from the get-go.) Everyone then puts a pin on the map where they live, a pin that will permanently symbolize their involvement in this healing experience. If time allows, we'll even play the Ultimate Koosh Challenge. If the kids can successfully toss the ball around the group fifty times without it hitting the floor, the group wins a fun prize. For instance, in a school program it might be a pizza lunch. In a church group it has been ice cream and a special video. In those locations where a pool is available, one of the staff must jump in the pool with all his/her clothes on. I have personally lost count—after 675—of how many times I've done just that through the years. This is a great way to get the group to come together quickly as a team. It works!

We hopefully establish a spirit of fun, comfort, caring, and safety before the "A" word, addiction, ever gets uttered. I begin by telling the group, "Everyone here has something in common. We all love someone who has had a problem with alcohol or drugs. So let's go around the group now to do introductions." Some youngsters truly have no clue who in their family has an addiction. That's how well it's been concealed from them. Others are just in complete denial as they claim no one or they speak about an aunt or uncle who smokes cigarettes. Still others not only admit who is addicted, but their pent-up words come cascading out in a stream of honesty. We let kids be exactly where they are during that first day. If they say they don't know, I tell them we'll figure it out as we go along. If a kid says, "No one in my family," my reply will be that we'll learn a lot over the next few days. This is a process, not an event. We have to let the process patiently unfold, as time is on our side.

I'll never forget the group with Tommy, Sophie, and Justin. While some programs prefer not to have siblings in the same group, I embrace the opportunity. Give them the chance to learn, grow, and heal together. Since they have experienced their family disease together, let them experience healing together as well. We consciously take steps to allow each to have his/her own experience. We set things up so they don't sit next to each other whenever possible, as side conversations only get in the way of the process. I also make sure not to allow siblings to answer for each other or do things for one another that each is capable of completing by him or herself.

So Tommy, Sophie, and Justin are all sitting by themselves as we embark on introductions. Tommy, the oldest at twelve, appeared somewhat resistant and disconnected when it was his turn to share. After many seconds of awkward silence he finally shared, "My mom said I could have a new video game if I do this program." We talked briefly about his favorite video games, especially those he has completely mastered. We weaved our way around the group, with many honestly naming who in their families was trapped by addiction. With the tension building and the room dripping with raw emotion it was finally Sophie's turn. This bright nine-year-old attempted to contain all her feelings, but her eyes welled with tears. "Sometimes Dad and Mom fight a lot, and I get upset and scared." While she didn't say who had the addiction, there was much more information and feeling than Tommy had expressed. I asked the group if any of them had experienced family fights, and most raised their hands in acknowledgment. Sophie was at least realizing that she was not alone in this regard.

Finally we made our way to Justin. Even though he was last, this seven-year-old sat on the edge of his seat and was ready to roll. "Let me tell you what happens at my house," he began innocently enough. I shot a quick glance in Tommy's direction and he was shaking his head in a disapproving manner, but luckily this seven-year-old was oblivious to that. "My dad goes into the bathroom for like an hour," he continued, "but he never flushes. I can smell smoke coming from in there, and I start getting scared." Everyone zoomed in on every word Justin shared. "Finally the door opens, and a mean, crazy alien comes out in my dad's body. Sometimes he hurts my mom and she cries. Tommy runs to get help, but Dad grabs him before he can." At this point Tommy is slumped in his chair with tears streaming down his face. It looks like he wants to run, but he's paralyzed by his little brother's honesty. Sophie has buried herself in one of our female counselor's warm embraces. The words keep pouring out of Justin, and he has the full, undivided attention of the group. "Sophie runs and hides under the bed. I go in the closet and refuse to come out until the alien is gone." Justin takes a deep breath, sighs, surveys the room, and finally locks in on me. "Hey, mister, will you please help me and my family?" We were off to the races.

From Risk to Potential

C hildren raised in families where addiction is present are at risk for a variety of behavioral, emotional, physical, and psychological problems as they grow and develop. They make up the number-one risk group for developing alcoholism, drug addiction, and other compulsive behaviors. Due to a powerful combination of genetics and environmental factors, all too often addiction becomes a family legacy that is inadvertently passed from generation to generation to generation. Where does it stop?

Children of Addiction (COAs) are also youth with great potential. Prevention and early intervention programs, whether offered in community or school settings, can provide children help, hope, and healing *even if* their loved ones continue on the destructive path of addiction. Such programs, offered at treatment centers, family service agencies, through the faith community, and in student assistance programs in the schools, empower kids with essential messages, skills, and strategies to cope positively with all the challenges they face at home.

The research on resilience consistently points to a critical factor for individuals who were able to rise above the hardship and adversity in their lives. That factor is the presence of a caring, nurturing adult. It isn't necessary to be a counselor to be that caring, nurturing adult. Perhaps more than anything else, I have worked tirelessly through the years attempting to be just such an adult for every youngster I have been blessed to serve.

Little Steps

It was a balmy 118-degree August day in the desert when a seven-year-old reluctantly strolled into the room for the first day of the children's program. With parents hovering around her like helicopters, this little one quickly made a name tag and quietly took a seat.

Mom and Dad said their good-byes, and for the next seven hours Chloe never took off the jacket that was zipped up to her neck. Despite sweating profusely, she kept that jacket on, hands safely tucked in the pockets unless it was time to eat or draw. It was a challenge to make eye contact and nearly impossible to coax a faint smile to her face. Her parents had warned me that she wouldn't talk about her mom's disease. Even though her mom had six months of sobriety and had taken her daughter to two different therapists, Chloe wasn't talking. Both parents were scared and disturbed about this.

On the second day, not much changed. Jacket on, hands tucked away, very little eye contact, no smiles. Even though she remained on the periphery of the group, Chloe was engaged and involved in every activity. At times like that I have to remind myself that children grow at their own pace, not when I think they should. It is so important to let kids simply be where they are and to honor and celebrate that. Everyone in the group accepted Chloe just the way she was, and while all of us gently and gradually took interest in her, we gave her space. When we played hide-and-seek in the dark that afternoon I noticed she had unzipped her coat and I actually "caught" her smiling. When Chloe noticed that I had noticed, her grin quickly disappeared. Little steps.

On the third day we were on the floor creating collages. Cutting, pasting, putting pictures and words on poster board. Out of the corner of my eye I saw Chloe crawling toward me, inching her way closer and closer. As only a seven-year-old can, she came right up to me and stuck her little face only a few inches from mine. Surprised, I didn't move. After several seconds of silently breathing on me, I finally figured out that maybe she wanted to ask me something. *C'mon, I've been clinically trained. This must be it.* I slowly moved my head back and whispered, "You can ask me anything you want. I promise, you won't get in trouble for asking. If I don't know the answer, we'll find someone who does." As she was just about to open her mouth—the moment of truth—she quickly scanned the room and saw that everyone was intently focused on the two of us. With a twinkle in her eye, she took off, crawling full-speed to the safe recesses of the unoccupied corner of the room with me in hot pursuit, excited that she was about to tell me something about her family or her feelings or a secret. *Breakthrough time, Yes!*

Alone in the corner, a wry smile came over Chloe's face as she took a few moments to collect herself. Then she gulped and sighed, and finally these words tumbled out of her mouth, "Where do you work?" This was one of the few times in my life I've actually been speechless. Chloe saw the confused look on my face and kindly reframed her question for me. "After you play with us on the floor all day, where do you make money?" I could tell she wasn't playing around; she was really serious. She was concerned about me, and I was appreciative.

Spontaneously, I blurted out, "I don't have a job."

She nodded sagely, and then an ear-to-ear grin filled her face. "That's what I thought," she said, gave me a hug, and raced back to the collage.

From then on I was just one of the kids, bigger than the rest, but someone Chloe could have fun with and trust. She worked hard, played hard, and didn't wipe the smile off her face for the rest of the week—and she never wore the jacket again. On the last day she talked about her anger, sadness, and hurt when Mommy drinks.

Why would I ever get a job after that?

❧

A Paradigm Shift: Strengths-Based Approach

For many years, the work with children from addicted families utilized a damage-model perspective: determine what's wrong and what's missing, and then attempt to "fix" things.

Unfortunately, this approach revolves around sickness and pathology. Far too many of these awesome children already deeply believe that something is wrong with them. Whether they get such a devastating message directly or indirectly from loved ones, or they simply tell themselves this, it weighs heavily on their hearts and dampens their spirits. This model may often reinforce the message that they are just not good enough. Some youngsters are inappropriately labeled with a mental health diagnosis so a therapist can work individually with the child to "fix" the damage. While some truly need and benefit from such therapy, my personal belief, developed through the years, is that there is great value in educational support groups helping most of these youngsters to learn, grow, and heal.

These boys and girls are survivors. Somehow, some way, they make it through highly chaotic, unpredictable environments where the rules often change and one never knows what will happen next. It often borders on the miraculous how they simply make it to school on a daily basis with all they must contend with and handle.

A strengths-based perspective helps kids realize they are special. I often hold up a "big mirror" in group to help children see the strengths, gifts, and tools with which they have been blessed. The objective is to help kids see these qualities, accept them, and deepen them to move toward a life of health and wellness. Such a paradigm shift, from a damage model to a strengths-based model, lets children also focus on what's right and develop pride in how they have made it through tough times in their life.

Therein lies the hope. So many have been caught up in all that's wrong, yet now can begin to see they have skills, tools, and caring adults to help them along the way.

A Different Perspective

Here was a huge dilemma that needed to be addressed and resolved quickly. A twelve-year-old girl didn't want to be in the program. She had a fixed scowl on her face, and the few words she did speak dripped with deep-dish sarcasm. Allison was the oldest youth in group, and this problem was compounded when another twelve-year-old girl canceled at the last moment due to a family emergency. Now there was no one close to Allison's age. I simply gave her lots of space that first day yet got absolutely nowhere the few times I attempted to engage her. I worried that her lack of connection and seemingly utter disdain for the process would spill out onto all the younger participants.

There was something about her that captivated me, but there was no way I could show it. I wanted her to remain, yet the unity and well-being of the group came first. Allison was a master at keeping everyone at a distance. While she doled out anger in many ways—sarcasm, silence, and disrespect—I saw a hurt and lonely young lady devastated by her dad's ongoing struggles with alcoholism. She was failing seventh grade, and her life was crumbling. With all this in mind I took a huge risk before the start of day two. I met with her privately and completely caught her off-guard. Thinking that I was kicking her out of the group, Allison was startled when I told her, "You don't have to be here if you don't want to be. I'll talk to your mom, just say the word." Allison put her head down and said nothing. "If you are going to stay, I need you to participate," I continued. "All of these kids look up to you, Allison, and they hurt due to the addiction in their families. They hurt a lot. I want you to be my leader. Let's help them feel better." She finally looked at me and just nodded. Lots of thoughts and feelings flooded her mind. She quietly got up and headed to the group room. As she walked away I hoped this would work and thought about the many times such a strategy hadn't.

It began almost imperceptibly, yet gradually Allison showed up and came to life. There was a natural-born leader deep down inside her that had been aching to come out. And, wow, did it come out. A youngster would share in group only to be met by Allison interjecting, "When I was eight years old, I would get scared, too, when my parents got into terrible fights." She'd look over to me for approval, look at the expression on my face, and then relate, "I still get scared about my dad's drinking." Allison also let herself play, and this was such a joyful sight to see. In the pool she taught Luis how to swim in only two days. After swimming one afternoon, I was at the right place at the right time. While they were putting their wet towels in the hamper Luis told her, "I've been praying to God for a big sister to teach me 'cause my parents are sick. God really listened to me." Luis hugged her with all his might, and I caught Allison's face as I was coming around the corner. She smiled, teared up, and held this seven-year-old, the little brother she'd never had.

Allison got real with her mom during the family sharing. She let out all the hurt and loneliness she'd been carrying for a long time. "Please love me, Mom. I'm sorry. I know I can do better. Please love me." At the end of the program Allison's mom was ecstatic about the transformation. I cautioned her that this was only the beginning, and continuing care for both of them was critical. Allison could have easily left the program, but underneath all her stuff were her strengths of caring and leadership, strengths that put her on a new path. What a gift that she could get in touch with them. Way to go, Allison!

Changing the Family Legacy

S ometimes the only difference between the children and the adults I encounter in my work is that the grown-ups never had a program to go to when they were kids. So many of them have a wounded child inside who needs to be loved, valued, protected, and respected. We give these parents and grandparents the same kindness, dignity, and caring the children receive. I have such admiration and affection for them because of their courage and strength in asking for help for their children and themselves. They are often giving their kids the gift they never received as a child— a safe place to grow, learn, play, and heal. The overwhelming majority of these adults know firsthand the pain and confusion of growing up in a family challenged by addiction.

Addiction robs everyone in the family. With the stress, chaos, and uncertainty, everyone is affected. When they are in the throes of their disease, alcoholics and addicts cannot consistently love the people who mean the most to them. Bringing their kids to a program for help is both a very loving act and an admission that their children have, in fact, been hurt. The last vestige of denial is admitting that addiction has hurt your children. This is a tough one to swallow.

Through the years I've heard all the excuses: my kids didn't know, they were too young to be affected, I only drank or used when they were asleep, I only did it away from them. I've watched many people in treatment really wake up one day and realize the disease they never asked for has not only hurt them but also their kids. For many this goes much deeper when they begin to have painful memories of growing up in a similar family as a child. Horror upon horror, this disease has been passed on to another generation. It's amazing to watch grown-ups begin to heal the little kid inside as they watch their own children embrace a path of healthy growth and development.

❧

The Kid with the Mustache

I had just talked about "Changing the Family Legacy" to a group with family members in treatment when a woman followed me out of the lecture and chased me down the hallway. I listened as this loving grandma described a very angry, confused, and hurt little boy who didn't understand why he couldn't be with his mommy. She was very concerned about her grandson, whom she was taking care of while her daughter was in treatment. At almost five years old, Billy was too young for the children's program that was an adjunct to the treatment center's family program. Nevertheless, Grandma advocated for some support and assistance for him with such assertiveness that I set up a family session.

Mom's drug of choice was methamphetamine, an incredibly destructive drug that wreaks havoc on all family members. She had been in and out of Billy's life, and this little guy had witnessed and experienced enough chaos, crises, and unpredictability to last a lifetime. As she watched her daughter self-destruct, Grandma became Billy's only reliable source of stability and love. Regardless of whether treatment would be successful for her daughter, I knew that Grandma was making Billy and his little sister her priority.

Billy was thrilled to see Mom again. He rushed into her arms as she entered the room, holding tightly to her neck as she told him how much she missed him and showered him with kisses. I settled on the floor for our thirty-minute session and began by telling Billy I was here to help him understand what has been happening in his life lately. Agitated and unsure, he watched Mom and Grandma, who sat with us in a circle.

I began by asking Billy if he went to school. "Billy goes to pre-school," Grandma offered.

"I'll bet that's fun, isn't it? Are you learning how to do all kinds of new things?" I asked.

Billy's large brown eyes moved from face to face until they rested on mine. "Uh-huh," he murmured.

"Well, I guess you've been wondering where Mommy's been," I began. He nodded.

"Mommy's in school, too, just like you. Only she's learning how to be a better mommy, one who doesn't yell, fight, or leave you. She is very safe here," I explained. "And you know what?"

"What?" he looked at me expectantly.

"Mommy talks about you every day." His beautiful brown eyes lit up and he smiled broadly.

"I miss my mommy," he said, as tears began to fall.

"I miss you too, Billy. Very, very much," Mom said as Billy crawled into her lap.

"What else does Mommy do at school?" Billy asked as his curiosity and confidence were growing by the minute.

"Mommy's learning not to use drugs anymore," I replied.

Fully aware of this painful reality, Billy exclaimed, "I like this school." Now Billy looked up at his mom and softly told her, "Mommy, I don't want those mean guys hurting you anymore. I can still make cereal for dinner," Billy proudly declared, "but I want you to stay with us. Please, Mommy, please." Then Billy looked at me and inquired, "Are you going to let bad guys hurt my mommy here?"

"No way," I replied.

After another long hug I asked, "You get to go home after school each day when you get your work done, don't you?" His little head nodded again as I continued. "Well, Mommy has to stay here at school until she gets all her work done. It's hard work and real important to learn, and it takes a while," I explained. "She'll stay here until it's time to go back home to be with you and your sister."

As we talked he became calmer and he asked some great questions. He drew a picture about his feelings and got quite playful in the process. He loved my giving him some high-fives and complimenting him about how smart he was. I captivated him with the many voices I could do, especially Cookie Monster and Donald Duck.

While Billy played, I talked to Mom about the importance of continued recovery, especially what a gift it would be for her kids, and I offered Grandma helpful suggestions about bedtime rituals, consistent structure, and discipline strategies for Billy.

By the time our session ended, hope had entered the room. Billy walked out with a bounce in his step, a smile on his face, and an occasional infectious giggle. Saying good-bye to Mom was still difficult, but he knew he'd see her again soon. He really believed this.

A small portion of caring and explaining can go a long way, even for a little kid so young.

On the car ride home Grandma asked this almost-five-year-old, "So, what did you think of Jerry?" Billy apparently got real quiet for several moments. Then finally he looked at Grandma with a scrunched-up face, appearing quite perplexed. "That kid has a mustache," he said, "but I like him anyway."

A Road Map

Children embrace, accept, and celebrate diversity better than anyone on the planet. While the kids and families are so diverse in many different ways and each program is shaped by this, there are a number of constants throughout the process. The first is to teach children about alcoholism and other drug addiction in an accurate, age-appropriate way. What a relief for youth to understand that it's not their fault, and they are not to blame. When kids fully realize that they can't make a loved one better, many have cried over this painful truth. By creating a safe and supportive environment for them, children begin to identify and express their thoughts, feelings, and concerns. In group they get in touch with their pain and learn a variety of ways to work through it.

In every children's program I've developed, kids also learn a variety of coping and self-care strategies. They are introduced to the important concepts of safe people and safe places. Every attempt is made to empower youngsters with healthy living skills and to use group as a safety net to assist kids in developing and deepening these tools. Lastly, children get in touch with their intrinsic beauty, goodness, and worth. Counselors reflect back to kids all their strengths and gifts, as well as facilitate activities that allow children to begin to heal and thrive.

Most importantly, children are given an opportunity simply to be kids. Play is an essential ingredient in the healing process. Wouldn't it be awesome if children could be kids while they are kids, so they don't have to be kids when they are adults? Laughter, fun, and play are an integral part of healing. Kids can play their way to health and understanding.

A Meal to Remember

He walked into the group room and cast a wary eye, especially at the few adults sitting in the circle with the other children. This nine-year-old wore a scowl on his face and herded his two younger siblings to their empty chairs with much skill and aplomb. He kept a watchful eye on them virtually every moment and was quite attentive to their needs, be it a tissue for a runny nose, a blue marker when they couldn't find one, or help in opening their juice containers. I was struck by how Timmy never smiled and yet what an incredible big brother he was to Ellie and George. It appeared that he had been doing this for a very long time.

Timmy, Ellie, and George were brought to the children's program by their foster parents. They were kind, caring, nurturing adults who had taken a genuine interest in these three who, underneath the surface, desperately craved love, structure, guidance, and positive attention. Their birth parents were both addicted to drugs, and their family life had been filled with chaos, unpredictability, and insanity. These three angels had been through way too much for any child to contend with and witnessed things—like violence, abuse, and severe neglect—that no young eyes should ever see. Despite all this, they really cared for these foster parents, as evidenced by the barrage of hugs and kisses they liberally doled out upon getting picked up at the conclusion of the first day.

Phil and Claire had been foster parents for years. When they took these children in about six months ago, Timmy, Ellie, and George were reunited, as they had previously been split up in their prior two placements. Phil and Claire sought out our program on their own as they could see the three desperately needed coping skills to deal with Dad's incarceration and the persistent worries that no one knew Mom's whereabouts for over a year. As Phil brought the kids in for our second day, Claire asked to speak with me briefly. "I don't know what you did yesterday," she began, "but all the kids could talk about going home was the program." I was amazed at this because they had said so little on the first day. I don't believe Timmy said three sentences throughout the day. He watched everything and everyone very intently, and Ellie and

George took cues from their big brother. Now Claire's eyes started welling up with tears as she shared, "Mornings are so hectic at the house just trying to get everybody up, dressed, fed, and ready for school. Today when I got up they were sitting near the door, all dressed and ready." As she sighed Claire continued, "They all raced over, hugged me, and declared, 'Hurry, hurry, we don't want to be late.' It was still an hour before it was time to leave."

In group that morning, Steffie spoke about the stepdad who hit her when he was drunk. The kids got very quiet as Steffie courageously told us what happened to her and then buried herself in a female counselor's warm embrace only to sob. When the time was right I looked at Steffie and told her that I felt sad and angry that this had happened to her. I could feel my eyes filling with tears as I emphatically stated, "It's not okay for a child to be hurt like that. It's not okay for anyone to ever get hurt like that." Timmy's hand instinctively shot in the air before he had a chance to think about what he was doing and stop himself. Now the others turned their focus and attention to this nine-year-old.

"I've been hurt many times, too," he began, as the words just started tumbling out of his mouth. "I've been hit many times like Steffie, but can I talk about getting hurt on the inside?" he asked the group.

"I'm so sorry this has happened to you," I offered. "Please tell us whatever you'd like."

Timmy took a couple of deep breaths, looked over at George, and then spoke his truth. "My old foster parents hurt me and

George. That's when we were split up and not with Ellie."

"What happened?" I gently replied.

"We were having a barbeque with steak, chicken, and corn on the cob. I was so excited because we never had a cookout before. George put a bunch of food on a paper plate, but the foster lady screamed, 'Put that back. There's not enough for you.'" Now Timmy started crying and shared, "She comes back out with a bowl of Cheerios for each of us. I wanted to yell, but I knew I'd get in trouble so I kept quiet. 'They don't give us enough money for you two so that's what you get.'" Timmy talked about how he just stared at his bowl and quietly ate the cereal. "George then started to cry, and she screamed at my little brother. 'Your family situation is all your fault. You misbehave all the time.'" By now most everyone in group was in tears.

Soon all the kids were looking in my direction. They could see that I was feeling angry, and I think they were actually glad about that. "That is not okay," I broadcast to the group. "I want the names of those foster parents." I looked at the other counselor, and we nodded in agreement for the group to see. "We'll do absolutely everything we can to keep you safe and protect you." What a group! What sharing! Such courage and strength from Timmy.

Timmy especially appeared lighter and playful throughout the rest of the program. That would not be the only time he took a healthy risk and let us a bit further into his world. As we came back from playing hide-and-seek later that day it was George who grabbed my hand and held it as we walked across campus. At one point I looked down at his angelic face, and I caught him looking at mine. As I smiled he simply said, "Thank you, Jerry."

Phil and Claire are such caring and nurturing adults. As for those other two, they are no longer foster parents.

CHAPTER TWO

Love Will Find
a Way

Breaking the Silence

ow it's time to check in with the family you met in "Only the Beginning" (page 3). They had just completed the initial four-day program. Angela, Brendan, and their father, Brent, were making huge strides in our sessions. With much courage and love, the children spoke from their hearts about how addiction had hurt them and their family. Even though both held back somewhat, they expressed confusion, fear, hurt, sadness, and anger in a gentle, sensitive way that deeply touched the spirit of everyone in the room, especially their father. We plant lots of seeds during our sessions, and I pray for a bountiful harvest for each of them. This was consistently being reinforced during their weekly hour-long continuing-care group.

On a beautiful spring day Brent, Angela, and Brendan went swimming at Grandma's nearby condo. Playtime with Dad was something they both expressed a desire for during our work. This was a very big deal for both of them. It had become a regular

occurrence over the past three months as the family navigated
through both the good and challenging times characteristic of
early recovery. What a huge gift to get the afternoon with Dad all
to themselves to splash around and have fun in the pool.

In the middle of swimming Dad casually said, "I'll be back in
just a few minutes." Angela and Brendan each shot a quick glance
toward one another but really didn't think much more about it as
the pool and laughter held their attention. Dad asked them to get
out of the pool and sit in the lounge chairs until he got back. A
pesky bee kept messing with both the kids, and Angela told her
brother to "go get Dad." Brendan, quickly approaching his seventh
birthday, went to search for the most important man in his life.
Quietly moving toward the condo and taking a peek in the window, the bubble suddenly burst for this precious little boy.

Brendan ran back to the pool to tell Angela what he'd witnessed.
There was no more carrying secrets for this youngster. "Angela, I
saw Dad drinking from a bottle," he shared with his big sister.
Angela did her best to calm him down and offer reassurance.
Brendan hoped that maybe it hadn't been alcohol in the bottle and
that everything would still be wonderful.

"I watched my dad pull out a bottle and start drinking," he told
me later, mired in sadness and hurt.

"Why would Dad do this? We were having so much fun
together. I don't understand. Please help me understand. Please.
When I saw my daddy coming back to the pool I knew the truth.
He was walking funny, and his voice sounded different." After
taking a deep breath this brave kid continued, "I was right in

front of him, but Dad yelled, 'Brendan, where are you?'"

Brendan related that he had many mixed feelings all at once. He was both really scared and happy. They all got back in the pool but Dad was acting wild. He was doing flips and somersaults, and acting like a kid. Angela would later remark, "He was acting like the dad I wish I had without the alcohol."

Brent gave his son a swimming lesson, yet it gradually turned sour. When Brendan didn't get the hang of it right away, Dad got angry at him. "His voice got real loud, and I looked at Angela. She nodded to me, and I kept really calm." The swimming came to a screeching halt in very little time.

When Mom got to the condo the kids took her aside to tell her what was happening. The last thing they wanted was any family conflict, especially between Mom and Dad. Judy listened intently to her children and quickly reacted with lots of emotions. This made it safe for the kids to feel their feelings as well. After lots of hugs, tears, and blown noses, Brendan looked at his mom and said, "I want to go back to the children's program. I still have lots of feelings inside of me. Maybe Daddy will want help, too."

Amidst all this anger, confusion, and sadness, Angela and Brendan were practicing many of the tools they had learned: not keeping bad secrets, asking for help, staying safe, sharing feelings in healthy ways. Despite the many family burdens they carried, they had huge smiles on their faces when they came back to the four-day program. These little children were filled with so much courage, strength, and hope.

Tapping In

L ooking around the room, there is hurt and pain every-where. The confusion and uncertainty are clearly etched on many young faces. Some are actually afraid of me and the other staff—unable to look at us or find a voice to engage in even simple pleasantries. How easy to get overwhelmed by the sadness that envelops the room! These children have been through so much in their short lives, yet today brings us all together for a new beginning. How I can best make a difference is all that really matters at this moment.

The gift is their presence. Today I get to meet them, work with them, teach them, play, eat, and do group with them. After just a few minutes my life has become quite enriched simply by having them in it, if only very briefly. I get to watch them courageously take the first steps in their healing. From a front-row seat I observe the thaw and watch an innocence, spontaneity, joy, creativity, and honesty slowly emerge. How can I best help them—simply love them along the way and create a way for them to love themselves.

God Blessed Me

I have such deep respect and admiration for adults who bring their children or grandchildren to a kids' program. It takes courage and strength to admit that one's children have been hurt by the family disease of addiction. It's an unbridled expression of love to allow youngsters a path of healing at such a tender age. One mom who recently brought her nine-year-old son to the program had eleven years of sobriety, and her son had never once experienced her active disease.

I had many initial reservations because I didn't want Phillip to be exposed to problems and situations he had never had to deal with in his life. In no way did I want any part of harming, confusing, or overwhelming Phillip in the name of helping him. I discussed this very openly and honestly with his mom, yet she was adamant about his participation in this prevention program, not only because of her family's long and pervasive history of addiction, but also to help him understand the importance of the recovery lifestyle she wholeheartedly embraced. She desperately wanted her son to get the gift of education and support she never got when she was a child. We agreed to take things a day at a time to make sure it was working for him in the five-day process.

Phil took to the program immediately and was a hit with his peers. He actively participated in all activities and listened most intently to the thoughts, worries, problems, and feelings of the others. He had a heart the size of a Ford F-150 truck. He'd tear up when others shared their pain, reach out his hand to anyone who needed it, and give astounding feedback with wisdom and conviction that belied his years.

The culminating event at the end of day two is for the children to write a story or draw a set of pictures about how addiction has hurt their family. It takes two full days to build trust, develop rapport, and deepen bonding to reach this critical point. The true magic of the process is creating a safe place for children to be with other kids who have experienced similar issues, challenges, and difficulties. Many understand for the first time in their young lives that they are not alone—other kids have gone through the same thing. Such a newfound connection runs deeply and powerfully.

At first, Phil struggled with this. He didn't have any stories to tell. He had never been embarrassed in front of friends by Mom's drinking, he hadn't been disappointed by broken promises or driven with a drunk parent. He squirmed in his chair, fiddled with his pencil, and struggled more as everyone else was writing away. I slowly approached his table, knelt down to be at his level, and whispered, "Just write about what you've learned here so far. Please consider it a blessing that you haven't had to go through much of what the others here have experienced." He nodded his head, grinned, and started to write.

The next morning, staff prepare the children and adults in separate groups for the children's sharing. The grown-ups experience a full range of emotions when they hear that the children are going to talk about the family disease—fear, guilt, shame, gratitude, joy, and sadness typically are discussed. Right before the sharing group, Phil's mom took me aside. "Maybe you were right in this being too much," she began. "I think it's time to leave." When I asked her what she was feeling, she just started crying. "I'm scared. I'm afraid my son will say he doesn't love me. I've worked so hard to get sober for the two of us that I know I haven't spent as much time with him as I'd like. I feel guilty." I encouraged her to stay. "You can't leave now in the middle of this. Let your son speak from his heart. I'll be there for both of you."

LOVE WILL FIND A WAY

Phil sat across from his mom in the middle of the circle when it was finally his turn. He politely declined to read his few sentences in favor of just talking to his mom. He started to cry before he could find the right words to begin. "I've learned one important thing here. God really blessed me when he made you my mom. Thanks for being sober for my whole life." Virtually everyone in the room was crying. "I promise I won't get mad at you anymore when you go to your meetings. Now I understand." They hugged and just held each other for a few minutes. This mom had scratched and clawed her way to recovery. What a gift her son gave her that day. This small family reminded me that the gifts of recovery can be bountiful in many, many ways.

Enter Their World

The best thing to do with children from addicted families is to develop a healthy, nurturing relationship with them. Kids don't care about how much you know until they know about how much you care. This requires counselors/group facilitators to truly "show up" each time they work with children and to pour their heart and soul into all their efforts. It's often the counselor/group facilitator who's the first adult in a child's life who consistently treats them with dignity and respect. Most of all, we need to love children; it's the best gift we can ever give them. Thankfully, I learned early in my career that love stands for:

Listen with your eyes, ears, and soul.

Observe how they live in the world.

Validate their thoughts, feelings, and experiences.

Educate and empower them with accurate, age-appropriate
information and healthy living skills.

Isn't it time to stop making children fit programs and instead make programs fit children? Historically, many COA programs took adult concepts and learning styles and tried to make youngsters adapt to them. Therein lies part of the problem. Many of these kids already grow up way too fast and are overburdened early with adult problems, worries, and concerns.

Let children be kids. Love them by giving them focused attention at every opportunity. Learn their names as quickly as possible. Repeat important stuff they've shared, at appropriate times, to demonstrate how you are really listening. Encourage them to ask questions, and when they need something, do your best to follow through. Don't just tell them they are important, but consistently show them just how much they matter.

Full Kid Status

Larry attended the children's program while his mom was in treatment at the center. He was an eight-year-old going on thirty, a very serious, no-nonsense youngster. Larry had a difficult time with all the pure fun activities such as swimming, hide-and-seek, ghosts in the graveyard, and kickball. If he couldn't somehow turn each into a competitive endeavor he seemed lost. He often stayed off by himself during free time and didn't engage in the playful banter during our lunches together. When another staff member announced it was time to play and I bellowed "Yes" in a silly fashion, Larry would roll his eyes and ask me incredulously, "How old are you?"

Larry had a great deal of responsibility around the house. His dad traveled extensively for work, and as an only child he steadfastly kept an eye on his mom, who was quickly spiraling out of control with her prescription drug addiction. He would often instinctively wake up three to four times a night to make sure that she was still breathing and okay. He often had to be the parent as no one else was consistently available to take on this responsibility.

During the family sharing Larry courageously revealed his feelings with his mother in front of the group, which included his father. "Mom, thanks for inviting me to this camp. It's mostly awesome here, and I'm learning lots of stuff. Me and the other kids have been talking about our problems," he began. "I love you the most but get scared that you're gonna die." With tears streaming down his face, Larry continued, "I have nightmares about it, wake up freaked out, and run in to make sure you're still alive." Now his voice started to rise as he blurted out, "I hate the disease you got. I want to kill it. Please get better." Mom clutched Larry as they both sobbed, releasing long-held, pent-up feelings.

After a few minutes holding his mom, Larry moved his chair back into the large circle. Dad reached out and gave Larry a long hug. Empowered by the experience with his mom, Larry looked intently into his father's eyes and spontaneously declared, "Dad, you're trapped by addiction, too. You won't admit it, but you are. Please, will you get help? I don't want to lose you either." Dad initially appeared dumbfounded, then started to sob. Larry buried his head in his father's chest, and they both cried. Mom sat quietly in disbelief, realizing that it was her young son who had the courage to break the family secret.

When you create a safe place and give children the chance to speak from their hearts without interruption, powerful things can happen. Dad went to the admissions department that afternoon to inquire about getting help for himself. He actually began treatment on the day his wife was discharged from the program.

A year has passed, and the whole family regularly attends our Children's Continuing Care Program on Wednesday evenings. Larry attends the seven-to-nine-year-old aftercare group while his parents participate in the concurrent 12-Step meeting. It's so gratifying to watch the family's growth, especially Larry getting to be a kid again.

One evening after group he frantically rushed up to me with exciting news. "Jerry, guess what? Next Friday night is my tenth birthday, and I can have a special friend come for the night."

He briefly came up for air, and the words shot out of his little mouth again, "We're gonna stay up real late, until about quarter to ten. There'll be pizza, movies, a candy stash; I got new batteries for my flashlight to look for night crawlers. I've stolen three rolls of toilet paper from the closet so we can TP out in front, ring the bell, and watch Dad flip his lid."

Before I could get a word in edgewise, he rushed on, "Will you be my special friend? Come over at 7:15 next Friday night?"

Larry had a gleam in his eyes and a goofy grin on his face. I was touched not only by his special invitation but also by the innocence and wonder he had recaptured.

By the way, we had an awesome time, but I didn't spend the night. My wife said no.

Create a Safe Place

I n her landmark book *It Will Never Happen to Me,* Claudia Black outlined the Family Laws of Addiction:

Don't Trust

Don't Talk

Don't Feel

Youngsters strictly adhere to these rules as a means of survival.

When children come to a program I ask them to do the exact opposite of what has allowed them to survive:

Trust me

Talk to me

Tell me how you feel

The miracle is that they do it. I'm always amazed how quickly this process unfolds, and the key is creating a safe place for the kids to express themselves.

Structure and consistency breed safety. Many of these children survive by always being a step ahead as they go through life. They pay a huge price in not simply being in the here and now.

Throughout the day I review the group schedule and announce what will be next. The effective counselor walks a tightrope of consistency and flexibility in the same breath, always willing to throw out the planned activity if something else comes along that is important and must be taken care of first. The key is letting the group know the change of plans. Positive group rules and consistently enforced consequences let the children know that their safety and well-being are paramount, and that you take this very seriously.

～

Way Beneath the Surface

He strolled into group an hour late. That first hour of the program is crucial to set the proper tone, get the participants all settled in, and demonstrate that this is a loving, safe place. While this had all been established fairly quickly, Franco threw it all out of whack in a matter of seconds. This twelve-year-old was dressed all in black and had a baseball cap tipped ever so slightly to one side, yet pulled down over his face. He wore baggy clothes and a number of gold chains around his neck. He slowly made his way to the empty chair awaiting him in the circle, slumped down into it, and crossed his arms with an air of defiance. The younger children appeared intimidated by this "gangsta" wannabe. My efforts to greet him were quickly met with, "Hey, nothing has ever happened in my family," which he hurled at me in a loud, angry tone.

Franco was initially very resistant to the process unfolding in group. While he refused to participate in activities, I could see that he was watching and listening to everything that transpired. I caught him paying attention a few times only to be met with his cocking his head back and rolling his eyes. Franco didn't want to play any of the fun games like hide-and-seek or kickball. He would stay off by himself, yet he took it all in. What he had the most trouble with was when other participants talked about family problems and feelings. When the emotional temperature soared in the room, he would squirm in his chair and mumble barely audible comments.

The second time he did this I gave him a consequence for breaking the "Respect Each Other" rule. Very gently, yet firmly, I told him, "Lucy is letting her feelings out right now, and you're interrupting her. She feels sad, hurt, and lonely about her mom's drug addiction and deserves to be heard. This is your warning, Franco. If you want to stay in this group, you must follow the rules just like everyone else. If you can't do that, you can't stay in this program. I would be really sad if you weren't here." The room got really quiet, as is usually the norm when staff dole out a consequence. Franco quickly nodded his head in my direction, shifted in his chair, and then stared at the floor. I was expecting some negative comeback from him and yet was met by his silence. Franco really had me intrigued.

Midway through the second day Franco raised his hand to share right after Eloise had painfully disclosed to the group she was convinced that her dad's alcoholism was her fault. I had no clue where this was going but couldn't resist calling on him, as he hadn't said a meaningful word since introductions on the first morning.

"I know exactly what you mean," he softly replied, looking right at the startled ten-year-old girl. "When I was seven I came home from school with homework. I asked my parents for help, and they got into a big argument about who was gonna help me and the best way how. My dad left the house angry, got drunk, and didn't come home for three days."

Everyone leaned forward and listened intently to each of Franco's words. Big tears rolled down his cheeks as he declared, "It is my fault. Yeah, it's my fault that Dad is an alcoholic. If I wasn't so stupid my dad wouldn't be trapped by alcohol." The group gasped at this assertion as Franco started to sob. "I'm so stupid, I'm so stupid," he kept repeating to the stunned group. Finally, the words he had locked so deeply inside came tumbling out, "I don't know how to read."

As he sat there sobbing and holding his face in his hands, Pedro got out of his chair, walked over to Franco, and put his hand on Franco's shoulder. Others quickly joined in as Franco had finally let down the many defenses he had so deftly used over the past few years.

At lunch, I took him aside and told him about an excellent program at school that could teach him how to read. A smidgen of hope was finally present in his life. Everyone in the group was learning in a new way that children don't make parents drink and use drugs, and they can't make parents stop. The participants looked up to Franco because he got real and told the truth.

On the last day of the program Franco actually got there early. While the baggy clothes remained, the ball cap and the gold chains had disappeared. I wish you could have seen the smile on his face when he played hide-and-seek and ghosts in the grave-yard with the rest of us. Franco was channeling all his inherent charisma in a positive fashion as he was in the center of all the fun and healing activities. He was on the right path, or so it appeared. He really got that it's not his fault and that he is very special.

Franco teared up at graduation as he wished the program "would never end." It was time for me to let go of him and the others, although they will forever remain in my heart and prayers. We can only hope that parents and grandparents take our continuing-care recommendations seriously. Six months went by ever so quickly until I found a letter on my desk. This is what was inside:

Dear Jerry,

Thanks for helping me. I am writing this letter myself. I know it's not my fault. I hope Dad gets help. I am now reading 5th grade books. I will never forget you.

Your friend,

Franco

Experiential Learning

When I hear something . . . I forget it

When I see something . . . I remember it

When I do something . . . I understand it

—Chinese Proverb

L earning by doing is the best way to reach and teach children from addicted families. Every person has a predominant learning style. Some learn best visually, some auditorily, others kinesthetically, and still others creatively through the arts. I'm always trying to gauge each individual's best learning style and adjust accordingly.

For COAs, words often have no meaning. "I'll quit tomorrow." "If your mom uses drugs again I'm divorcing her." "This is the last time I'll ever take money out of your piggy bank." "I'll be back in twenty minutes. I just need some cigarettes." "I'm sorry I hit you, but I'll never do it again."

In group, we always initially move beyond words. Experiential activities can get people out of their heads and into their hearts, which allows for deeper levels of insight, understanding, and access to feelings and emotions. Rich and varied activities, such as stories, TV game shows, art, puppets, role-play, music, games, and play lend themselves to this process. Create opportunities for kids to be active participants in their healing and discovery. Then always allow ample time for discussion as every child will have a unique perspective on each activity, and the group is enriched when they all share.

The Stampede

I frequently get calls from professionals who want advice on setting up a children's program. Most know that they want to teach kids about addiction in age-appropriate ways, to help them enhance their communication skills by identifying and expressing feelings, and to empower them with coping and self-care strategies. Many want to include a focus on helping youngsters build self-worth and celebrate their strengths. While these are all essential ingredients, one simple thing often gets overlooked: creating the opportunity for children to be kids.

Way too many children, consumed by adult responsibilities and worries, grow up too fast in addicted families. Effective programs provide a balanced blend of learning and fun. Through play, youngsters complete crucial developmental tasks and develop important social skills. Games and fun represent a critical part of the healing process. A child may share something significant and take a huge leap in their healing during lunch, the walk back to class, or while playing a game. You never know when that moment may take place.

The challenge is finding the appropriate games to play to match both the mood of the group and the often limited space available. When we do school groups, activities such as Head's Up, Seven Up, Koosh Ball, the Telephone Game, Nerf Garbage Ball, and Neighbors can work very well. The weather can make it necessary to stay indoors, so these activities can again fit the bill. Sometimes reading a fun story to the group, setting aside time for jokes, or playing hangman on the board can be effective options. We always try to make the space work best for everyone.

We sometimes play hide-and-seek in the dark in the children's program if we have the blessing of a larger space to work in. Whether it's in a church basement, hotel conference room, school auditorium, or state-of-the-art lecture hall, the space quickly transforms into a children's playground by shutting the drapes and turning off all the lights. Children love this game: the thrill of the chase, the exhilaration of tagging base free, and the camaraderie of working together in joyful pursuit of winning.

Hide-and-seek is a tough game for me because I'm stuck with my adult body, but I try to hide well and force the person who is It to find me. When we held one particular group in a huge auditorium with seats bolted to the floor theater-style, there weren't a lot of places to hide myself. Well, I got the idea to hide between two rows of chairs, and I crammed my body as close to one row as I possibly could and rested my head in my arms on the floor.

Some kids use hide-and-seek time to run around and blow off steam, but in this particular game everyone remained hidden and silent. I must have nodded off to sleep (it's exhausting keeping up with these kids every day!) because all of a sudden I was surprised by a runaway freight train. Laura stepped on my legs, back, and head as she ran down my aisle. Next came Steve, Cyndi, Phillip, and Frank. All I could think to do was relax until the stampede was over. Carli, Tyler, and Ronnie came next. Frankie almost tripped as both of his feet balanced on my head as he was moving at top speed.

Marylou stopped her hot pursuit, tagged me (I was the only person tagged that game), and incredulously stated the obvious, "What a stupid place to hide!"

❧

Embracing Diversity, Touching Hearts

I'm grateful to have worked for treatment centers that serve individuals and families from around the globe. I've been fortunate to travel and work with children from addicted families in Russia, Japan, Australia, and China. While the key is always touching people's hearts, it's also imperative to understand, embrace, and incorporate cultural differences to respect and honor those we serve.

Always ask the experts to guide you in making your approach fit those you serve. Professionals from different cultural backgrounds have helped me immensely to modify and adapt activities and the appropriate manner to present and facilitate them. While I couldn't speak their native tongue or learn everything I really needed to know about cultural differences, it was these caring professionals who guided me in touching kids' hearts. They provided helpful suggestions and introduced me to important stories and traditions that strengthened and deepened the relationships I was developing with the kids.

Kids are kids all around the world, with many more similarities than differences, yet it's important to allow these differences to be an integral part of the work.

~&

Lupé's Treasure

Every so often, something happens that reminds me of the impact our children's program has on the lives of the kids and their families. I always try to be a caring, nurturing adult in their lives, sadly often the first grown-up who has related to them in this loving manner. Many walk in that first morning with big hearts that have repeatedly been disappointed and broken. Even though some initially keep their distance and stay heavily defended, they desperately need to be listened to, understood, validated, and loved. Lupé was certainly one of these kids. This eleven-year-old looked like a mother hen as she guided her two younger brothers through making name tags, putting all their gear in adjacent cubbies, and finding three empty chairs together in the circle. Although quiet and reserved, Lupé's beautiful face featured a huge, radiant smile that could immediately steal your heart.

These three come from a very poor family, the poorest of the poor. While Mom spoke very little English, she was a powerful lioness when it came to protecting her children. She put herself at great risk by enrolling her youngsters in the program without their dad's knowledge or approval. This was a risk she was very willing to take as her children's safety and well-being always came first.

Lupé and her brothers were quite blessed in this way. They got a ride each day from the kids' social worker, as this family didn't even have a car. They listened, learned, ate, and played like there was no tomorrow.

For the first two days Lupé had very little to say about her dad. My sense was that she loved him so much and was conflicted about telling the bad things he did in the throes of his alcoholism and drug addiction. Some children remain pretty tight-lipped due to fear of reprisal if their parents get wind of what they talked about in the program. This wasn't the case for Lupé, as the love she possessed for her father was evident during the first morning's introductions. Lupé's two younger brothers made up for their big sister's reticence and then some. Ernesto, age eight, spoke at length about Dad often staying out late and spending all the money on drugs and alcohol. Arturo, the little guy at almost seven years old, drew a very revealing picture of his parents' fighting during the art assignment near the end of the first program day. The younger kids are, the closer they are to the truth. Make it safe, and their words, art, stories, and role-playing will reveal exactly what is going on.

When it came time to share and discuss the artwork the next day, young, brave Arturo spilled the beans. "One time there was a big fight," he began, "so Lupé took us in the back room to be safe. I heard a loud crash and a door slam. I was really scared." All three of these siblings started crying as Arturo explained, "My dad hurts my mom. She was crying and bleeding. My dad was gone." Arturo got out of his chair, raced across the room, and landed in his sister's lap for her reassuring embrace. Ernesto wasn't far behind.

As I wiped away my tears I wondered how many times in their lives they had done so.

Lupé had been gently moved along this entire process by Carole, an awesome children's counselor. Carole encouraged Lupé to speak the words she had locked inside for so long. Carole explained to Lupé that it was time for safe adults to help her be a kid again. When she sat across from her mom for the sharing exercise, this beautiful, strong, amazing eleven-year-old dug deep and poured out her heart and soul. "I get scared when Daddy hurts you, Mommy. If you get hurt so bad, who will take care of us? I don't want to go to a foster home." Mom reached out and tightly clutched her daughter as they both cried. I held Arturo's and Ernesto's hands as I sat between them on the outside of the circle. They cried, too.

Mom made it clear on the last day she would keep her children safe. Lupé, Arturo, and Ernesto believed her, as was evident by the relief and joy on their faces. We even worked on a safety plan for the family and promised to find the right help for Dad if he ever asked for assistance. Right before graduation Lupé took Carole aside to talk privately. "Thanks for helping me," she began. "I don't ever want you to forget me." Lupé pulled out a well-loved, ragged old bear and presented it to Carole." I've had him since I was really little. Now I want you to have him. Thanks for loving me." That bear sits quite prominently in Carole's office. It was a huge gift from a child who had so very little. Yet what she and her family did possess, such love and caring, were truly in abundance.

Have Fun

An important goal of group is that children actually want to come back and keep on participating. There has to be something there that intrigues and excites them, something that they are not consistently getting from other people and places in their lives. A child-centered focus, based on dignity and respect, goes a long way toward creating such an atmosphere, but it isn't quite enough in and of itself. A balanced blend of fun is essential to seal the deal.

Many COAs have lost the ability to embrace fun, joy, and silliness in their lives. Some never had this ability, as trauma, loss, and pain at a young age made it impossible to develop such skills. Counselors need to bring their heart and soul to the "party" and to let their passion and enthusiasm run loose. There have been innumerable times where youngsters have gone from joy and laughter to tears and pain in a heartbeat. Let the children play, and be playful with them along the way. Simply creating a safe place where these precious children get to be kids for just a little while can foster bonding, trust, and closeness that can't be fully developed in any other way. Enjoy the journey, for it is such an adventure and gift.

Neighbors

Within the first ninety minutes we typically play a fun game with children called Neighbors. This little game serves so many important purposes all at the same time. First, it simply allows children to be kids, as it's pure fun and enjoyment. Second, it gives youngsters the chance to speak to the entire group in a playful way. Many youth find their true voice in the program, and this is one way that it all begins. Third, they get to run around and burn off some of the nervous energy that's been gnawing at them. The group members sit in their respective chairs in a huge circle. There is always one less chair than people playing so someone is always It in the middle.

I start off first, declaring, "All my neighbors wearing a name tag, move now." Every person with a name tag then gets up and races around the room looking for an empty chair to sit in. Someone else, who didn't find a chair, is now It, and they declare, "All my neighbors who are wearing sandals, move now." People not wearing sandals stay in their seats, but those wearing sandals scramble around trying to find an empty seat. Kids love this easy game and want to play it all the time.

For those first ninety minutes I take most of my cues from the children. If the group is especially quiet, I'll do lots of the talking. If they are very chatty, then I'll listen. If they get really silly, often due to their defenses, I become serious in a gentle and kind way. Sometimes the group starts out way too seriously as some youngsters don't know how to play and have fun. This is when I get really silly to break the ice so they can see they don't have to be perfect or act like an adult here. One group especially began this way.

I patiently bided my time until we played neighbors. I thought maybe this would mix things up a bit, but wow, was I wrong!

Children were throwing out such statements as "All my neighbors who love math," or "All my neighbors who detest hot weather," or "All my neighbors who enjoy sushi." Finally I was in the middle, and I knew I really had to rock this boat. I took a deep breath and declared, "All my neighbors wearing Scooby-Doo underwear, move now."

At first, silence filled the air; perhaps it was actually shock. Muffled giggling started emanating from all corners of the room, only to be followed by robust laughter. When no one got out of their chair I deadpanned, "C'mon, I can't be the only one here wearing Scooby-Doo underwear." The group squealed with delight. "Kid" energy filled the room.

I followed by responding, "All my neighbors who have ever picked their nose, move now." Zach bolted out of his seat, yet was perplexed that he was the only one to do so. He quickly looked around the group and blurted out, "But I never eat it." Yup, we were right on track.

◦❦◦

Double Rainbows

It usually takes about an hour for children to warm up to the program and feel safe. When the group is filled primarily with six and seven-year-olds, the process often speeds up. It doesn't take long to see the deep bonds and affection these boys and girls have for their parents. Despite all the challenges posed by alcoholism and other drug addiction, as well as all the related problems that often accompany it, most kids love their parents with all their hearts and souls. It's amazing to watch young children sigh, sit up in their chairs, nod affirmatively, and smile when they realize and accept that their parents are good people.

As this pride grows, particularly for children whose parents are committed to treatment and recovery, youth vocalize it in a variety of ways. A chorus of "My mom is a doctor; my dad's a lawyer; my mom is an accountant; my dad is a teacher," often fills the room. Johnny, a talkative seven-year-old not about to be left out in this discussion, loudly declared, "My dad drives a truck with eighteen wheels. I know, I've counted each and every one of them." Donna, a sage six-year-old, offered, "My mom has the most important job in the United States of America." Against my better instincts I went for the "bait" and asked, "What does she do?" With a wry smile, she announced, "She takes care of me." The room erupted into giggles and laughter.

At lunch one day a monsoon dumped about a half inch of rain in twenty minutes. The skies got dark, and thunder and lightning put on an unforgettable, dazzling show. Mother Earth was in full beauty and splendor. As the children came back to the group room I was preparing an activity about identifying and expressing feelings. It was time to get to work on this.

Helene excitedly came running into the room describing the beautiful rainbow she had just seen stretched out across the mountains.

"Let's go see the rainbow, Jerry. It's so beautiful."

Without hesitation I replied, "No, it's time to practice letting our feelings out." We were behind in the program activities, and I wanted to get to this critical part of the process.

Soon I realized the unpopularity of my declaration.

"Please can we go see the rainbow?" Chad requested as politely as I've ever heard him. Claps and cheers filled the room.

"It's important to work on our feelings now," I shared in an attempt to get the group back on track.

Carlita, a tiny eight-year-old, raised her hand as tears gently rolled down her cheeks. When I acknowledged her, she stated quite seriously, "But it's a double rainbow. I might never get to see another like it."

She had stopped me in my tracks, but she wasn't even finished yet. "I've kept my feelings inside for a long time," she continued. "I don't think ten more minutes will matter that much," she eagerly told me.

I certainly couldn't argue with that logic, so we headed out to marvel at that double rainbow.

I can still vividly recall its beauty and the looks of wonder on their faces. Sometimes I wonder who are truly the teachers and who are the students. A double rainbow. Whoa.

CHAPTER THREE

Simple Lessons

Just for Today

L et's catch up with Brent, Judy, Angela, and Brendan again. In "Breaking the Silence" (page 31), you experienced their ongoing struggle in overcoming the family disease of addiction. As you've seen, Brent and Judy are dedicated to breaking the cycle of addiction in their family. Many parents have the best intentions of keeping their kids involved in the healing process, yet few regularly follow through on a weekly basis. Brent and Judy did. The kids were in separate continuing-care groups based on their respective ages, and their parents were actively involved in the concurrent 12-Step meeting. Week by week, the children deepened their insights, strengths, and healing as the collective recovery of the family grew rapidly.

Both children would usually greet me with a smile on their faces and a bounce in their steps. Each, in their unique way, related the peacefulness and joy they now felt with their family and the gift of spending fun times with their dad. Angela, typically quick with a heartfelt hug, would whisper, "Addiction isn't anywhere near my house." Her eyes would dance with joy, and she'd quietly gaze at her father with pride. The times were good, and the future appeared to hold only more of the same.

Gradually Angela embraced this newfound joy. Nevertheless, a part of her remained on guard, keenly watchful and slightly worried. She was the oldest and often cared for younger kids in the family when things got chaotic and crazy. As a result, she possessed more insight, felt things more deeply, and had experienced more of those terrible times when it all suddenly unraveled. When I observed this subtle side of her emerging, I gently reminded her to live just for today. These words made a deep impression. She quickly flashed a wry smile in my direction and nodded affirmatively. I'd mention "today" virtually every time our paths crossed. It became a game for us, our secret code. Angela was letting go the best she could for a ten-year-old child and focusing on caring for herself.

Play days, dinners together, vacations—this family grew closer than it had ever been. Sometimes Brendan would be so full of excitement recounting all the cool stuff he had been doing with his dad and family that he couldn't contain himself. He'd bob back and forth from foot to foot and couldn't get the words out fast enough.

So few children from addicted families learn how to care for themselves. It's certainly not that they aren't capable or competent; it's just that no one has ever taught them, and they haven't had many role models practicing this. In the children's program, we play a game called Jeopardy, the Self-Care Game. Parents and children brainstorm self-care strategies for five areas: body, mind, feelings, spirit, and kid. Once complete, everyone decorates their own self-care bag and writes down ideas for each category using index cards. Angela loved this activity and took special interest in thoughtfully picking out care ideas she'd enjoy and filling out the cards. She was excited about regularly using the bag just for herself.

Then one day the call came, around 4:30 in the afternoon. Many kids phone around that time of day, as they haven't been home from school for long. Angela's voice was quivering and cracking with emotion, and I instantly knew something was seriously wrong.

"Dad's drinking again," she began and then suddenly stopped, overcome by a turbulent sea of emotions. "He started fighting with Mom, but I stayed safe by going to my room."

Before I could offer a word of encouragement and support she declared, "I went right for my self-care bag and pulled out a card. I know I can't take care of my dad or mom, but I really want to right now."

We talked for a long time while she expressed hurt and confusion that addiction had trapped her dad again. Most of all, she talked about fear. "I'm scared that Dad might never get better, and I don't want to lose him."

When the time was right, I simply said, "Today. Focus just on today." Our secret code seemed to help diminish her fear. I told her how very proud I was of her and that I'd be around to listen and help her any way I could. Before we ended the conversation, Angela said thoughtfully, "When I reached in my bag, the card I pulled out said 'Talk to Someone You Trust.' Jerry, thanks for helping me today. I love you."

As I hung up the phone, I closed my eyes and prayed that Angela, Brendan, their parents, and family would stay safe. Just for today.

~ॐ

Breathing Space

fter working with them for years, I've learned a great deal about how to serve these children and their families effectively. At the top of the list is to remember always that less is more. These are little kids—often seven, eight, nine, and ten years old. Most have been through way too much in their young lives. For many, it's more than the challenges of alcoholism and drug addiction, as some must also contend with violence, maltreatment, financial hardships, divorce or separation, a loved one's mental health problems, and parental incarceration. They can get overwhelmed by all these difficulties and really need help to get through.

When boys and girls come through the doors, I want to give them love, education, support, tools, strategies, and safety. Whether you work with children just one hour a week, conduct a weekend retreat, facilitate a four-day or five-day process, or run a summer camp, it often seems like there will never be enough time. It's imperative not to overwhelm these awesome kids all over again by trying to accomplish too much in your programs.

Slow down. Let them breathe and bask in the environment of love and safety you've created. Bonnie, age nine, offered a huge compliment in this regard. "I really love it here," she began.

"How come?" I queried. "This is the one place in my life I can do this," Bonnie continued. She sat down in her chair and let out a huge sigh. She smiled and nodded in my direction. I understood exactly what she meant.

Healing is a process—give children a reasonable portion each time you meet. Provide ample opportunities for them to digest all the "goodies" you serve them. Let them ask questions, have fun, and practice their new skills.

Kylie's Truth

Despite all the struggles and turmoil that frequent families hurt by addiction, the overwhelming majority of the children still love their parents. They want their parents to get better so these dads and moms can spend time with them, care about them, and play with them. I'm continually amazed at how children summon up the necessary courage to talk with their parents about their hurts and sadness.

I remain in awe of the strength of the love that children have for their parents and the bravery that children possess to speak the truth. It just goes to show how a Higher Power truly guides this miracle. Kylie, all of seven years old, couldn't even do a story about what had happened to her family as she was starting to learn how to read and write. This minor obstacle surely didn't hinder this determined girl as she suggested in group that she would make some pictures for her daddy instead.

When it was Kylie's turn she didn't hesitate to join her dad in the middle of the circle. She showed her first picture of herself crying and said, "I never got to say good-bye before you left. I was scared you might never come back." With her chin quivering and eyes filling with tears, her voice got real soft. "I love you, Daddy. Please get better." Everyone in group lost it, especially her mom, who had tricked herself into believing that her little girl hadn't really been affected. Kylie had spoken her truth and let her feelings flow. Not only had she deeply touched her parents but also everyone else in group. By going first, Kylie set an example for the other children to openly and honestly talk with their moms and dads as well.

As we made our way to lunch after group, I ran into Kylie and told her how proud I was of her for what she had just done. Within a few seconds she took hold of my hand as we entered the cafeteria. I took a deep breath and reflected on my many blessings. Suddenly, Kylie stopped in her tracks and tugged hard twice on my hand and arm. I spun around, knelt down, and looked into her deep blue eyes. Without hesitation she said, "Jerry, how long have you been at the Center?"

Without giving it any thought I quickly replied, "Seven years."

Her little jaw dropped and a look of confusion filled Kylie's face. She stared at me for a few seconds, then offered, "Wow! You must have lots of problems. My dad only needs to stay here for thirty days."

⎯⍦⎯

What Kids Care About

A nother powerful lesson I've learned—which I mentioned earlier—is that kids don't care about how much you know until they know about how much you care. Most children from addicted families are emotionally hungry for love and attention. They desperately want nurturing adults to take a genuine interest in them. Perhaps the biggest tragedy of this insidious disease is that it prevents alcoholics/addicts from consistently loving the people who mean the most to them. Many youngsters silently wonder if they are good enough and really matter. Just giving these kids a little focused attention goes a long way to initiating the healing process.

A program can have engaging toys and gadgets. It may possess the best evidence-based curriculum. It can have an unlimited budget for all the latest bells and whistles. Yet none of this will matter unless the facilitators bring their heart and soul to group every day. Programs don't heal people. It's people who touch others' hearts and deepen healing. It's the kindness and caring of the leaders that leave children with a clear message: "I really matter." It's taking the time to listen; to watch a little one jump in the pool for the eighty-third time; to reassure them when they've spilled an entire glass of milk on the carpet; to help them, yet again, to tie their shoes; to let them express their anger without fear of reprisal; to give them a fair, reasonable consequence when their behavior is inappropriate.

I'll never forget the little boy who had to have a green folder when we had run out of them. He didn't want to be in the program to begin with, so this was the frosting on the cake. One of the staff, who wasn't working this particular program, was heading out to purchase supplies for an upcoming retreat. I told her, "Whatever you do, come back with a green folder." I promised this eight-year-old I'd have a green folder for him by lunchtime. His only response was to declare, "Yeah, right." I couldn't help but wonder how many promises had been broken in his short life. When I gave him his green folder a smile spread across his face. This simple act was a turning point for him.

While this requires lots of energy and stamina, these children truly deserve nothing but our best.

Hey, She's My Sister

He came bouncing into the room, full of energy and enthusiasm that was infectious and joyful. Cody could barely contain himself as his laughter and playful banter naturally drew everyone toward him. This small eleven-year-old completely adored his sixteen-year-old sister, who served as his mentor, role model, and protector. Long before we ever got to introductions, the whole group knew that big sis Tammy had been to rehab and had been clean from drugs and alcohol for over five months. Cody was so very proud of her.

While most youngsters come to the program as the result of a parent getting trapped by addiction, it's not uncommon to serve children whose older sibling has the problem with drugs or alcohol. While the circumstances might be somewhat different, the family dynamics and feelings are quite similar. It became crystal clear that Cody felt scared, guilty, shame, and hurt as a result of his sister's addiction. He was especially rocked with fear that she might relapse. "Are you positive there's nothing I can do to prevent Tammy from relapsing?" he asked the staff on the first afternoon during the Addiction game. "I lost my sister once, and I don't want to go through that again."

Cody hadn't yet experienced his growth spurt, so he could be an easy target for bullies. While he kept his wits about him and could humorously diffuse most potentially explosive situations, it became clear that Tammy had bailed him out of many difficult moments. She was beautiful, wore the latest fashions, and was really cool. Cody benefited from her status, and it became a part of his status as well; heck, he was Tammy's little brother. All was good until addiction wreaked its havoc on this family and drove a wedge into their close relationship.

As they sat face to face for the sharing exercise, they both started sobbing once they peered into each other's eyes. Cody was so afraid to tell his sister the truth about her disease, concerned that it might hurt her so much that she'd start using drugs or drinking again. Tammy loved her brother more than anyone on this planet and didn't want to go anywhere near how her addiction had hurt him. Both courageously walked through their fears and realized that this exercise was the best thing they could possibly do.

"I thought I had lost you forever, Sis," Cody could barely get out in a whisper. "I got so scared that I had done something wrong to hurt you, and I never want to do that. I love you." With these words, Tammy really lost it because she knew in her heart how much she had hurt Cody with her drug addiction. "Most of all, I was hurt and mad when you stole my gold chain and sold it for drugs. Sis, Grandpa gave that to me." Tammy looked bewildered and perplexed. While she nodded her head, it was clear that she didn't have a clue. At the conclusion of this process I asked Cody if he had anything else to tell his big sister. "No one could ever take your place. I need you. I need you, Sis. I need you." Cody climbed right into her lap and threw his arms around her, something that he had done many times before in his life.

Tammy found me later and declared, "My disease got its butt kicked today. I really needed that. This has been the best thing that's happened to me since rehab. I don't remember taking that gold chain. I must have been in a blackout." Realizing just how critical her continuing care was, Tammy shared, "It must come first. I never want to see Cody's pain like that again. I want him to always be proud of me and look up to me."

Let Them Play

he American Academy of Pediatrics (AAP) released a 2007 report on the importance of play. The report details how free and unstructured play is healthy and essential for helping children reach important social, emotional, and cognitive developmental milestones, as well as helping them manage stress and become resilient. Many children from addicted families grow up too fast as they become consumed by adult roles and responsibilities way beyond their years. Some are devoured by grown-up worries, problems, and secrets, sending the typical hurried lifestyle most American youth already face through the stratosphere.

When it comes to working with children from addicted families, play typically gets short shrift. It's so easy to get caught up in that "not enough time" syndrome that the importance of play gets diminished. It's essential to strike a balance here. Hide-and-seek, capture the flag, ghosts in the graveyard, even tossing a Koosh ball around the circle are fun games that boost trust, bonding, and teamwork. Swimming provides a great release, as unstructured time in the pool allows the use of imagination. Play provides excellent opportunities for children, in a safe environment, to actually practice and deepen the very skills they're learning in group: communicating, problem solving, setting boundaries, and asking for help. It teaches youngsters a great self-care skill and stress management technique. Make the time to let the children play.

❧

Bathroom Breakthrough

Years ago, I was asked to facilitate a children's program during a national conference on children of alcoholics. This four-day, all-day program was open to the children of conference participants who had a history of alcoholism or other drug addiction in their families. It was a novel idea, but I had no clue about what was to transpire.

The conference took place at a posh hotel in downtown Chicago. Staff had set out puppets, crayons, magic markers, stories, games, and other assorted props before the kids arrived. It quickly became clear that many of the participants, primarily the boys, didn't want to be there in any way, shape, or form. The ringleader, a savvy ten-year-old, quickly put it all into perspective. "Put the puppets away. We don't do crayons. We don't want any sad stories. Wipe that smile off your face, Opie" (no doubt a reference to my resemblance to Ron Howard, especially strong in my younger days). It was at moments like this that the management trainee job at Jack in the Box, in retrospect, looked really appealing.

Well, we were off to a great start. I remember looking up at the clock and thinking that we only had five hours and forty-five minutes left on the first day of the program. It was time to throw out all that we had planned for the day, enter the childrens' worlds, and create a safe place for all. It was a long, hard day, but we held on to just a tad of hope.

Day two actually went better and we made real progress, although the boys kept testing us throughout the day. We held firmly to all the group rules and predetermined consequences, and everyone eventually fell in line. The biggest gift was that they all showed up and participated. There were occasional giggles and laughter as well as a few glimpses of self-disclosure, albeit guarded at times. It's easy to forget that this is a process—that it doesn't all get completed in a day or two. Little did I expect the breakthrough would be so sudden and unexpected.

Things went smoothly at the start of the third day until it was time to take a break. The boys and girls headed off to the bathrooms on the third floor of this luxury hotel, not far from our assigned group room. The young ladies came back quickly to enjoy the morning snack, and we got deeply involved in a discussion about relapse. When I finally realized that the boys hadn't come back, I looked at the clock to see how much time had gone by. Fifteen minutes, certainly a red flag. Time to send out a search party of one—me.

The most ornate bathroom I've ever been in is the one on the third floor of that memorable hotel. Six shiny sinks all in a row. No levers there. Simply stand in the right spot and the water comes on automatically. Huge, long mirrors with lights all the way around to make things bright. No paper towels, just fluffy white minitowels for the hands and face. Enough free toiletries available to easily take care of the needs of a small city. As I approached the bathroom all I could hear was the distinct sound of running water. These tough "mini-adults" were standing in a line by the door next to the first sink. One by one, each boy strolled down the row, stepping in the right spot to make all the sinks flow with water simultaneously. Joy filled their faces as they high-fived each other when they ran back to the starting line to begin again.

They weren't sure how to react when I walked in. I caught them red-handed. They were busted. Without uttering a word I quickly went to the front of the line so I could be next. They shouted, hollered, and cheered me on. Laughter filled the restroom. We kept playing for at least another five minutes. The "kid" part of these children had finally showed up. It dramatically changed the dynamics for the rest of the program.

Allow Them Their Pain

T hese children not only contend with alcoholism and/or other drug addiction every day but also the related issues like fighting, broken promises, neglect, and verbal violence.

Youngsters tend to hold it all in, but the load often becomes so large that it seeps out in many different ways. Some act it out behaviorally. Others manifest it physically as the unresolved stress leads to headaches and stomachaches. Still others appear to hide it well until they come to a safe place with safe people and other children who've gone through similar experiences. In healthy, balanced ways, children need to let go of all the stuff they've been carrying around. Many come to realize that they've been lugging around their parents' stuff and their family's stuff as well. It's time to let go.

The recipe is quite simple. Create a safe environment where kids are loved and respected. Whether verbally, or through art, stories, role-play, or writing letters, they start to express themselves. It actually becomes contagious as they spur each other on. Some begin the minute the program starts and others take a few sessions, but virtually everyone engages.

Let the children have their pain. Hurt, anger, loneliness, fear, sadness, shame—it will all start to come out. The key is to be around their pain without trying to fix it. It's not unusual for children to express guilt about parental addiction and family troubles. Facilitators often want to jump in and emphatically implore, "But it's not your fault," Let them simply feel their guilt or other emotions and just work through it. Express it, be with it, experience it, get some validation, and then release it. The key is simply being with the children, connecting with them, and experiencing all of them.

⁓⁂

A Few Words ... That's All It Takes

Elle hadn't spoken more than three dozen words over the first twenty-four hours of the program. This twelve-year-old was fully immersed in all aspects of the five-day process but just choked up full of emotion every time she tried to speak. The other kids were quite kind and understanding as they offered words of encouragement and smiling glances and clamored to sit next to her at lunch.

It was time for graduation, the last hour together, and the adults slowly made their way into the group room. As Elle's dad, a patient in treatment, entered the room, she stood up and spontaneously declared, "There's my dad. He's my dad." With pride etched upon her face and dripping from each and every word Elle continued, "He's an alcoholic and addict. It's not my fault. It's not his fault. Addiction has been hurting our family for years. My grandpa died of it when my dad was a little boy." A hush came over the room, and the dad froze in place as his daughter shared for all to hear.

Tears quietly fell from his eyes. When Elle saw this she couldn't hold hers back any longer. "Oh, Dad, I just thought you didn't love me anymore. I didn't understand what happened to you, but now I do." The silence was broken when the adults in the room started clapping. Elle hurried across the room into her dad's arms, crying tears of joy while Dad's were a bittersweet mixture of gratitude and sadness. He was grateful for being in recovery today and having his daughter completely back in his life, but sad that he never got to do this with his father.

During the graduation ceremonies children receive a certificate, a recovery medallion, an affirmation book, their first newsletter, and ways to stay in touch with staff, including an 800 toll-free telephone number, and e-mail and snail-mail addresses. When Elle was honored, she momentarily stopped the proceedings to say a few words. "Thanks, everybody. All this stuff is great. I met so many new friends and had a great time here. But the best gift I got today is that I got my dad back." This time Dad raced over to her for a long, heartfelt hug. Once again the room quickly grew silent as virtually everyone grabbed another tissue.

Bob had been through treatment programs multiple times but just couldn't stay sober. The longest period he had ever stayed abstinent was ninety-seven days. Elle's heartfelt words proved prophetic as they led her father down a new road to health and wellness. He had never spoken much about his dad in treatment, never exploring his unresolved grief, not only about losing his father at such a young age, but also having only memories of a drunk dad. After the program that day he wrote a long letter to the father who couldn't be there for him as a child. He shared it and deeply emoted in his grief group. This lifted a huge burden off Bob's shoulders and empowered him to step up and be the dad for Elle that he unknowingly had longed for all his life.

I recently got a Christmas card from Elle. On the cover were her three beautiful kids. Joy filled all their faces. The photo inside featured her dad skiing with his grandkids. True to form, Elle wrote only a few words:

Thanks for showing me and my Dad the way. I'll never forget the gift you've given us.

Love,

Elle

Flexibility

I t is an arduous task, but essential, to always be willing to throw your whole plan out the window, change course midstream, and develop a new avenue to best meet the needs of the group in any given session. Remember, we are making programs fit children, not making children fit programs.

When it comes time to pick the "right" activity for group, it's humbling. I find this especially true with continuing-care groups, as these youngsters have already spent at least twenty-five hours acquiring a common base of knowledge and skill sets in the program.

In planning for this hourly group I'll often tell myself that with all my infinite wisdom and experience, I know exactly what activity will work well here, only to find myself in the middle of an activity with seven- and eight-year-olds when that little voice echoes in my head with a resounding, *It's not working!*

I keep deluding myself and proceed. Finally, *mayday, mayday, crash and burn; bail out, get out, stay out,* goes off in my brain. I'm often the last to know (or accept) that the activity isn't working as the kids realized this eight minutes ago.

Stop and switch gears. Let the group know you're going in a different direction. Always have a backup activity or two ready to go. Change course whenever necessary. This will be a huge asset in reaching the kids and families you are to serve.

Camp Crisis

Throughout the years, the consistent and effective staple for working with children of addicted parents (COAs) has been the weekly educational support group session. No matter if this takes place in a school (as part of a student assistance program), the faith community, a recreation facility, a community center, or in a treatment program, children from addicted families benefit greatly from the care and nurturing of group facilitators, an engaging program of activities, and the safety created by being with peers who have experienced similar problems, feelings, and concerns. Whether it's thirty minutes, forty-five minutes, or an hour in length, it simply works the best for the most COAs.

Using the weekly session as a solid foundation, I've experi-

mented with other models as an adjunct. Weekend retreats afford
the opportunity to facilitate a variety of more in-depth activities.
Kids' Kamp, a six-day, five-night experience that still operates to
this day, was born in 1985.

Summer camp was upon us again, and the staff had prepared
accordingly. We had planned well with lots of options, and time
had suddenly become a luxury. There would be plenty of chances
to connect—during meals, group, and free time. It wasn't until I
arrived at camp that I received the bad news. One of the leaders
was ill and wouldn't be coming. Now I had to quickly rethink
everything on the fly. All I was really concerned about was the start
of camp, as I had learned in years prior just how critical it was to
set the proper tone right from the get-go. I knew many kids would
be saddened by the news that a favorite leader would be missing,
and we would need to process before we could move on. This
leader had always been at each camp and played a huge role in its
success. The children would really miss him.

Now was the time to be flexible, so I completely switched the
opening activities. I wanted to address this sudden dilemma before
anyone noticed, wondered, and asked questions. Here was a gift,
although I certainly didn't initially perceive it as such, to allow
everyone to talk about the situation and hopefully share feelings in
the process. For many youngsters from addicted families this
would be virgin territory as family problems aren't often acknowledged, let alone addressed. In silence, youngsters wonder what's
happening and tell themselves a story so it all makes sense.
Unfortunately, such a story often includes the assumption that the

child has done something wrong to create the dilemma. Today we could do it differently.

So there we were: thirty children and six staff plus three junior counselors. After brief introductions I got right to the business at hand. "I've got some bad news, and I feel really sad right now," I began. I let the group know what was happening, and virtually no one was at a loss for words. The floodgates opened and emotions poured all over the room. At first the youngsters acknowledged anger, hurt, loneliness, confusion, and worry. Sensing the mood, a ten-year-old offered, "Maybe he'll make it later in the week."

"No," I countered. "We tell the truth here. He won't be coming to camp this year at all."

I reflected on what a loss this was for everyone there. We talked about what losses are, and I invited the kids to share some of theirs. They bravely talked about friends moving away, the death of a pet, or special possessions disappearing. The room grew very quiet.

Franklin put a new spin on this discussion. A bright and perceptive twelve-year-old, he offered, "Growing up with addiction you lose lots of stuff." Many heads nodded around the circle. Manny added, "I lose time playing and having fun with my dad when he's on drugs." Devon chimed in, "I've lost many friends who've come over to play. They see my dad drunk and acting crazy." With tears in her eyes, she continued, "They're not allowed over at my house anymore." Cheryl shared last. "I'm the oldest. I have to take care of all the younger ones in my family when my parents get trapped. That's why I love camp. I get to be a kid here."

The group was wide open, and this start far exceeded my expectations. We actually ran thirty-five minutes over, yet there was no stopping this discussion. So we didn't get to everything planned. We still had five days left. Here these precious kids were trusting, talking, and feeling. For many it was the first time in their young lives that they handled a difficult situation in a healthy, balanced way. They were given accurate, age-appropriate information, and afforded the opportunity to ask questions, share feelings, and relate this to other aspects of their lives. It set the tone and atmosphere for an incredible experience, as we reflected back on the concept of loss throughout our time together. While every camp has many special moments, this Kids' Kamp has always been the most memorable one for me.

CHAPTER FOUR

The Rock Garden

Sad and Happy at the Same Time

A call came at 2:45 AM on December 22. I had the beeper, as it was my turn to take Holiday Hotline calls. Every year we offer a hotline for kids during the two weeks of Christmas/Hanukkah vacation. This is often a very challenging and difficult time for children from addicted families, as the holidays bring extra family stress, tension, drinking, drugging, and conflict. I called the number and was startled out of my sleepy repose. It was Judy. There had been a single-car crash, and she requested that I come to the house to help tell the children that their dad Brent had been killed.

Brent was a good man, husband, and father. He had gone through the program twice with his kids and faithfully got them to the continuing-care group most Wednesday evenings. While he struggled with his own addiction at times, he had a strong conviction that he'd get his kids the help he never got when he was a young boy. He once told me, "I'll do anything to spare my kids from the insanity of my childhood. I don't want my children to hurt and be confused as much as I was." His voice started cracking with emotion as he declared, "I don't want them to get this disease."

I arrived at the house about 6:30 in the morning, joining family members shocked and saddened by the inexplicable turn of events just hours before. I offered Judy my condolences and promised to be there for her and the kids.

As the sun came up, signaling the dawn of a new day, I sat quietly watching the children peacefully sleeping in the family room under the Christmas tree they had put up and decorated the evening before. I couldn't help but think about how their lives would never be quite the same after they awoke.

With strength she didn't know she possessed, Judy did a masterful, heartfelt job of telling her children that their father had died. "You know how much Daddy loves his truck," she began. "Well, he was driving it yesterday when there was a terrible accident, and God took Daddy back home." She struggled to compose herself as she continued, "He's safe with God now. Daddy doesn't hurt anymore, and he will always be watching out for us."

A look of confusion and sadness crossed Angela's face as she and Brendan listened carefully. "I know how proud he is of each of you. Daddy always told me that. And even though he's with God now, you can never, ever forget how much he loves you." There was nothing more Judy could say. Sobbing and tears filled the room. Each of us took a turn holding and consoling these wonderful children. I kept reminding them what a special person their dad was and how much he loved his family. Sometimes it's not the words, but being physically, mentally, emotionally, and spiritually there for the children that matters the most.

An hour or so passed when Angela told me that she wanted to talk because she had some feelings to share. She led me into another room so we could be alone for a few minutes. This bright, gifted ten-year-old told me that she had two feelings to share.

"I feel very, very sad because my daddy is gone. I would give anything if I could have just one more day with him." I held Angela as she just sobbed. She was letting the rocks out of her bag.

Finally, she looked at me with her puffy, red eyes and declared, "I also feel happy."

This completely startled me; it was the last feeling I was expecting her to share as she had just lost her father.

"Jerry, I feel happy because addiction can't hurt my daddy anymore."

I could feel my eyes quickly filling with tears and responded, "Angela, where is your dad now?"

She smiled, pointed a finger upward, and stated, "He's in heaven. My dad was a good person, but sometimes the disease made him do bad things."

"What's your dad going to do on his first day in heaven?" I wondered out loud.

"He's going to an A.A. meeting and then to play golf," she replied with innocent conviction. She had it all figured out.

I still see the kids regularly, and Angela tells me she still misses her dad dearly every single day. But just as it did that day a few years ago, her comfort comes in knowing that her dad is finally free from the clutches and ravages of that insidious disease.

∽◆

The Bag of Rocks

I t sits innocently in the center of the group. Youngsters initially have no clue that it actually weighs forty-one pounds. Each child gets the chance to carry it from one end of the room and back. Everyone struggles to carry it in their own unique way. Some pretend it's no big deal, but you can see the struggle on their faces; others lift it up for a few steps, put it back down to catch their breath, and repeat this process over and over again. Still others drag it across the room. Almost all agree life would be miserable if they had to carry it all the time. They would become tired, grumpy, grouchy, and not even want to get out of bed. It would interfere with having fun and friends. Kids relate that they'd always be thinking about the bag and just want to get rid of it.

We help children to see that their moms and dads have been carrying around a heavy bag like that. It's on the inside, close to their hearts. Kids learn that their parents have been collecting "stuff" in their bags since they were little kids themselves, so it couldn't be the kids' fault. The bag gets so heavy that some people drink alcohol or use drugs to temporarily put the bag to sleep. When the substances wear off, the bag actually gets even heavier. Drugs and alcohol don't solve problems; they make bigger ones.

When people develop addiction they need to get help. They go to counselors and treatment centers to learn how to deal with all the stuff by letting it out of the bag, one rock at a time. The bag passes around the group, and each child takes out a rock. Each rock represents feelings like angry, scared, hurt, lonely, and guilty. There are problems such as addiction, fighting, and abuse. There is also the secrets rock. The rocks stay on display for the entire program as they guide the journey. What do we do here? We learn about problems, share feelings, and, if kids ever want to, let out secrets. The children begin to take rocks out of their own bags.

God's Hands

They walked in holding hands, a dad and his little girl. The deep love they shared was etched on their faces, but it slowly became apparent that a chasm was growing between them. The girl sat in a chair, and her hands quickly disappeared into her pockets. She tilted her body away from her dad's, and silence filled the room. Dad nervously tapped his foot on the floor and scanned the room, looking for clues as to what might unfold over the next four days.

Kelly was a bright, engaging nine-year-old. Her mischievous smile lit up the room, and she loved to play and be silly; she was also sharp and focused, and she effortlessly stayed half a step ahead of the group process. Everyone in the group quickly came to care for her and include her in everything we did. She really connected with the others, who helped her get in touch with deeply buried feelings.

Kelly's dad, Mike, had just celebrated one year of sobriety. He had been struggling to reach this milestone for over eight years but kept getting tripped up by the seductive disease. Mike was filled with guilt and shame as he painfully realized how each relapse had hurt his daughter. He hoped for a better life for them and knew that his recovery was riding on it. He desperately wanted a closeness with Kelly that he had never experienced with his own father, who ultimately died of his alcoholism when Mike was only twelve.

On the third day, it was time for Kelly to share with her dad. Facing each other in the middle of the group they both started crying before either could utter a word. As she read her story she conveniently left out the most emotionally charged incident that had hurt her so badly and continued to impede their relationship. I wasn't surprised. When I initially asked her to share about that scary morning she instinctively shook her head no before I could get the words out.

When Kelly finished reading, I asked Mike if he wanted to hear all of his daughter's thoughts and feelings. Puzzled, he looked at her and softly pleaded, "Please tell me. I really want to know."

Kelly took a deep breath and began. "I woke up on a Saturday morning and found you lying on the floor. When you wouldn't move I called 911, just like the other times. When the paramedics arrived, they tried to help you but I heard one of them say, 'It's not looking good.' I thought you were dead." Kelly's tears came from a place deep within. While her dad appeared dumbfounded by this revelation she continued, "I don't want to lose you, Dad, but I can't take this anymore. I'm scared I'm gonna lose my daddy." They embraced for several minutes as they both sobbed.

Kelly and Mike went home with renewed hope and a simple family plan. A few weeks later, Mike called to report they were becoming closer, but that Kelly was experiencing awful nightmares. She worried about her dad at bedtime, afraid that his addiction would trap him again, and she actually checked on him during the night. Going back to her therapist was very helpful, but Mike sensed something was still missing.

Despite the five-hour drive, in a true commitment to their discovery and recovery, Mike brought Kelly to see me once again. Kelly wasted no time sharing her anxiety and fear that the disease would capture Dad again and that maybe next time she wouldn't be there to save him. That was the crux of Kelly's dilemma. She would feel anxious and fearful yet couldn't do anything to really help her dad.

I asked her to close her eyes and visualize God's hands, particularly how huge they must be. A wide grin spread across her face as she did this. I encouraged her to put her dad directly in God's hands any time she got scared about addiction grabbing him again. After all, God could protect him better than anyone or anything. When Kelly opened her eyes she looked relieved. I took a beautiful oak box off my shelf and handed it to her. She saw the two words on the top and uttered, "God Box." I had bought this box years ago at a conference and found great comfort in regularly using it to let go of all the stuff in my life I couldn't change. Now it was time to pass it on.

"Before you go to bed at night, write down any problems or feelings you need God's help with and put them in the box. Write down any people you especially want the Creator to protect while you are sleeping," I told her. She gave me a strong hug, and that mischievous grin reappeared on her face.

That was four years ago. Mike has now been clean and sober five years. He has never been closer to Kelly and cherishes every day he gets to spend with her. I'm told she still uses that box from time to time. The nightmares have gone away.

~

How Do You Feel?

A major goal when helping children from addicted families is for them to express their thoughts, concerns, and feelings. Many adults make the erroneous assumption that these kids already know how to identify their feelings. It's been my experience through the years that many of their parents, most of whom also grew up in families challenged by addiction, have little experience in identifying a full range of emotions. For example, some can only name three or four feelings they've ever experienced. Much the same holds true for children. They typically have not been growing up in families where they are encouraged to share feelings or have role models in identifying and expressing emotions in healthy ways. It's essential for youth to learn about feelings first.

Many years ago, a psychologist from Russia spent five days training with me in a children's program. She taught me much more than I ever taught her because she simply questioned almost everything that happened during the process. She was completely new to this and offered a fresh perspective. Her queries helped me deepen and strengthen my approach to making a real difference in these kids' and families' lives. She wondered why there were no visual cues on the wall to help youngsters identify and express their feelings. What a fabulous idea! The very next day feeling faces were up in the group room. No, not that poster with sixty-four feeling faces that asks, "How are you feeling today?" Just eight to ten feeling faces.

Since that day, every group room features feeling faces. I've even created activities about them, like the land of feelings place game in my book *Discovery . . . Finding the Buried Treasure.*

Forgiveness

Justin is the youngest in his family. He is a remarkable kid who came into the program with a smile, rolled up his little sleeves, and worked intently throughout. This eight-year-old lives in a "looking-good family," where trouble and stress lurk just beneath the surface.

On the third day of the program Justin stopped me with a very anxious look on his face. "Will you please come with me to my dad's group this afternoon?" he nervously asked. "I don't think I can do this without you." As his eyes watered, I gave him a hug and told him I would be there for him every step of the way. He faced the daunting challenge of going into his dad's group and

telling Dad how addiction has been hurting the family. To compli-
cate things further, all his family would be present, including his
grandparents.

As we headed toward Dad's group, Justin grabbed my hand and
held it tightly. "You can do this," I reassured him, yet he blurted
out, "I'm scared, Jerry." I knelt down to be on eye level with him,
but before I could offer words of encouragement, Justin explained,
"I don't want to hurt my dad and mom."

"I don't want you to do that, either," I agreed. "Just tell the truth.
Tell on addiction." He got a wry smile on his face, nodded approv-
ingly, and told me to hurry up.

Justin did a masterful job of letting his dad know how much he
loved him yet how much he hated Dad's alcoholism. The group was
moved to tears during this eight-year-old's courageous sharing. Most
of the participants had also grown up in families hurt by addiction,
so they could easily relate to Justin's poignant words and manner.

When I asked Justin if he had anything else to share, the tears
finally started rolling down his cheeks and his bottom lip began to
quiver. He looked right at his dad and declared, "Stop hurting my
mom. You hurt her when you hit her and call her names." Justin's
words rocked the group, but he still wasn't done.

"You call me bad names, too, and I get scared of you, but I still love
you." With these final words Justin reached out and melted into his
dad's arms. It took an eight-year-old to bust the family secret: domes-
tic violence. After the two of us left, that group had lots to work on.

On the last day of the family program it was time for the forgiveness group, and Justin and I were invited to attend. Soon after we

arrived, Dad asked his son to join him in the middle of the circle. It took Dad several moments to compose himself before he could talk to his little boy. "Son, will you forgive me for calling you names, not spending time with you, and hurting your mom?"

Justin immediately blurted out, "Yes, I forgive you but only on one condition."

I had prepared Justin for this process, but he was veering off course.

"I forgive you only if you play with me twice a week." The group erupted with laughter, and Dad promised to do just that.

Then Grandpa invited Justin's dad out to the middle. Chills went up my spine when this seventy-one-year-old man spoke to his son. "Will you forgive me for not spending time with you, calling you awful names, and hurting your mom?" It was as if Dad and Grandpa had written up their forgiveness lists together. You could see and feel how the trauma and abuse had been passed along to each generation.

Dad started to cry as he heard the words he had been longing to hear for so many years and finally replied, "Yes, Dad, I forgive you." They embraced and just held each other.

Justin's dad made his way to the outside of the group, but Grandpa couldn't move. Finally, he put up his hands to cover his face and sobbed. Gently, I asked this man, "Sir, why are you crying?" He looked up and softly replied, "I just forgave my dad."

It was a child who led the way. Just for today, the generational cycle of addiction, trauma, and abuse had been interrupted.

The Elephant in the Living Room

W hen it's time to talk about addiction, you can sense the fear and trepidation in the room. Many are simply scared that it really is all their fault. Some get told this either directly or indirectly, while others just reach this conclusion on their own. To best meet the unique learning style of the children in group, it is critical to utilize a variety of tools to shed light on this disease. I always prefer a combination of stories, film, art, and games. The real magic in the process for kids is being in a room with others who are going through the same things—similar problems, worries, and feelings. Here youngsters may finally realize that they are not alone.

I've made numerous references to the Addiction game throughout this book. The Addiction game, unlike any other activity I've used, teaches children in powerful ways. Here you take the abstract concept of the disease process and make it very concrete by personifying addiction. A facilitator role-plays the disease so kids can hear it, watch it, react to it, and have feelings about it. Youngsters get to hear Addiction tell all the lies and set the trap to take control of the addicted person's life. Here, kids experience a powerful visual as they come to separate the person they love from the disease that consumes them. Slowly they understand that it's not their fault, and they also begin to develop ways to avoid this trap as they get older.

Bringing Mom Home

"There's absolutely no way that's ever going to happen," she blurted out in an angry tone. I could clearly hear the emotion building in her voice. The mere suggestion, delivered in a careful, gentle manner, that her son might have been adversely affected by her problem drinking was too much for her to hear. Sitting across from me was a bright, attractive thirty-four-year-old physician who wanted to be anywhere else in the world besides my office. She was intent on setting me straight that her oldest child had not only never been affected but also would *never* be participating in a kids' program. "Sammy has absolutely no clue because I would only drink at night while he was asleep in bed," she asserted. "I don't want you to be filling his head with a bunch of ideas. He's only eight." She glared at me and declared, "I am a good mom." I shook my head affirmatively as she bolted out the door.

The last vestige of denial is admitting the disease you never asked for has not only hurt you but your loved ones as well, especially the children. What person in their right mind would ever hurt their children? This is such a painful place to go, yet perhaps the denial was slowly cracking for this proud, caring mother. About five days after our initial encounter she watched the kids from the children's program coming back from swimming. They had smiles plastered all over their faces as they were laughing and giggling about "throwing" me into the pool that particular afternoon. Even she couldn't hide the smile as she witnessed me dripping from head to toe. These were awesome boys and girls, full of strengths, hopes, and dreams.

Something touched her as she watched them parade by. "Can we meet again?" she asked as I passed. "How about at 4:00?" I suggested. "I should be fairly dry by then."

Her mood and tone had softened considerably. She began by stating, "Don't you think eight is awfully young? He really doesn't know about any of this." I knew she was genuine as her face was filled with emotion.

"Where does your son think you are right now?" I asked.

She quickly teared up upon hearing these words and offered, "He thinks I'm working." She paused, but before I could get a word in edgewise she continued, "But I've never been gone this long." Sadness quickly enveloped her as she was looking at this situation in a brand-new light.

"Did you grow up in an addicted family?" I asked thoughtfully.

"Yes, but it was so different with my mom and her drinking. There was yelling and fighting, and she never had any time for me." She was starting to get all worked up as she asserted, "I am not like that in any way. There's no yelling, and I spend lots of time with my children."

I purposely interrupted by offering, "Could you have benefited from a program like this when you were eight? Would your life have been better at such a young age?"

This stopped her in her tracks and was met with stone-cold silence. "I gotta go now" was her only reply.

Sammy's dad had agreed with his wife that the children's program wasn't a good idea—until his son brought home a note from his third-grade teacher one Friday afternoon. She was very concerned about Sammy because he didn't seem like himself at school. He was so sad, withdrawn, and distracted. This caring teacher wanted to know if anything was happening at home that was troubling this bright boy. As Dad read the note he knew it was time to immediately take action. Once the two younger ones were put to bed, Dad explained to Sammy, "Mom isn't away working right now. I just didn't know how to tell you. She drinks wine after you go to bed at night. Sometimes she drinks too much and it makes her sick. She's at a special place getting help. I'll take you to see her on Sunday."

Sammy wouldn't say a word and his face looked expressionless. After many moments of awkward silence he softly uttered, "Dad, I'm going to bed now."

Dad was awakened early the next morning at about 5:30 as he heard a loud commotion downstairs in the kitchen—cabinets opening, doors slamming, someone talking to himself. What could this be so early on a Saturday morning? When he entered the kitchen he found Sammy fully dressed. He even had the hood on from his sweatshirt. Sammy had a flashlight in his right hand and a handful of Fruit Roll-Ups in his left.

"What in the world are you doing?" Dad asked him. "Sammy, it's the middle of the night!"

Sammy turned toward Dad and shared, "Dad, I'm going to get Mom now and bring her back home."

Dad was startled by his son's words. With tears streaming down his face, Sammy said, "Oh Dad, I'm sorry. I didn't mean to tell Mom I hated her when she wouldn't let me go to my friend's house. I'll do better in reading and I'll clean up all the dog poop and won't fight with my sisters anymore. I just want to tell Mom I'm sorry I stress her out and make her drink." Dad held his son and they both cried.

Later that day, during their phone call, Dad told his wife all about what Sammy had done. This touched her in a very deep and tender place. When I got to work the next morning, this mom was anxiously standing by my office waiting for me to arrive.

"I want to sign my son up for the next program," she declared.

"Absolutely," I excitedly replied. "You are giving your son the gift you so desperately needed as a child. You're changing the family legacy."

"I just love my kids so much," she shared.

"Yeah, I knew that from the moment I first met you."

Treatment and Recovery

When these special kids learn about addiction it can sometimes be a mixed blessing. When they understand that their loved ones are trapped, children often break through any remaining denial. Like many adults, it's especially tough for them to come to grips with the fact that they can't make their addicted family member better, as these kids would do virtually anything to see their loved ones get well. On the bright side, they realize that it's not their fault and that they are not alone. In an effort to build upon hope, we introduce children to "Treatment" and "Recovery." T&R are the arch nemeses of addiction. They help people get better, and they come in many forms, including treatment, counseling, 12-Step meetings, therapy, and a turn to faith. Once the alcoholic/addict asks for help or accepts it through a form of intervention, T&R come to the rescue and provide a safe haven to ward off the disease.

Children and families can truly heal if they make T&R an essential part of their lives on a daily basis. Through counseling and educational support groups, at both community and school locations, children from addicted families can learn to be kids. They can have fun, develop new interests, and engage in a multitude of activities. They can learn new ways to help care for themselves and stay safe. They are able to communicate their thoughts and feelings to people they trust. These children can find safe people and places to help them. They can feel good about themselves and develop strengths, even if their loved ones continue to be stuck in their disease. They can celebrate who they are and move forward to have a good, balanced life despite what is happening in their families.

Call Grandma Now

Tessa was an adorable five-year-old who stole my heart the very first moment I met her. She had bright blue eyes, curly blonde hair, and a radiant smile that could magically light up the room. Most Thursdays she wore her jean overalls and brown sandals, her little uniform for the four- to-six-year-old group she enthusiastically participated in on a weekly basis. She initially came to the program when her mom entered a treatment program for alcoholism. I always looked forward to this particular group.

With four- to six-year-olds we always kept things pretty simple.

It's essential to make the program fit the children and not the children fit the program. Hence our weekly group met for forty-five minutes. After a twenty-minute introduction and creative activity we took a short break for water, the bathroom, and a rousing game of follow the leader as we traipsed our way throughout the treatment center, clapping our hands, barking like dogs, or slithering like snakes. This gave us fifteen minutes for a brief discussion and closing. Since there were only six youngsters max in this group, every boy and girl received lots of individual love and focused attention.

Tessa took to the process immediately and always shared with great gusto. I'll never forget what she had to say during just her second session in the program. "I don't want my mommy to be sick anymore," she told the group. When asked how she could tell when Mommy was sick, she said, "That's way easy. She stays in bed, sleeps a lot, is very grumpy, and yells at me." Tessa took a deep breath and stated, "She forgets about me. My mommy forgets about me." All the others rallied around her when Tessa started crying. She was able to stay in this group for six months as it was written into her mom's continuing-care plan. At her last session she handed me a little gift that was beautifully wrapped: a Bugs Bunny figure on a key chain, a gift I've treasured to this day. It was hard to let her go, but I was excited about the new life she'd begun with her mom.

Eighteen months passed and I hadn't heard any word about this family. One day Tessa, now a second-grader, came home from school, took one look at her mother, and declared, "You've been drinking that yucky stuff again."

Despite Mom's vehement protestations, Tessa asked, "Well, what's in that glass?"

"Diet Coke," Mom replied.

Before Mom could get there first, this seven-year-old took a big sip, ran to the sink, and spit it out. She did, in fact, taste that "yucky" stuff in the glass. With hurt, anger, and disappointment surging through her tiny body she silently glared at Mom, went to her room, and slowly shut the door. Mom, apparently dumbfounded, was not sure what to say or do.

Tessa came out twenty minutes later carrying her backpack and clutching her Care Bear. Her backpack was full of clothes and her prized treasures. She slowly walked up to her mom and softly said, "Please call Grandma now. Mommy, I can't live here anymore. If you keep drinking that yucky stuff you are going to die." Mom collapsed on the couch as a result of her daughter's simple yet poignant words. Tessa wasn't done yet though. "Mommy, I love you, but I don't want to be here when that happens. I'll wait outside. Bye, Mommy."

Before Tessa got to the door Mom took her daughter and held her ever so tightly. Within minutes Mom was on the phone. Within an hour she was back in rehab.

Self-Care

Children from addicted families often get so caught up in the family problems that they forget about themselves. Many focus on the addicted person and hope the drinking and drug use will stop. Others worry about the nonaddicted spouse and fear that a separation or divorce may be looming. These children have few role models of individuals taking good care of themselves. Everyone gets stuck on the high-speed, unpredictable roller-coaster ride of addiction.

Years ago I created a television-like game show to teach children and families about self-care. It's a little like *Jeopardy* and a little like *Wheel of Fortune,* so I called it Jeopardy Wheel, the Self-Care Game. The five categories are body, mind, feelings, spirit, and kid. These are all important ways to be good to ourselves daily. With a spin of the wheel to determine point value, children and parents brainstorm ways to care for themselves in all five categories. Everyone shares their self-care ideas in the group.

Next the participants decorate self-care bags. Once they are satisfied with their custom-made creations they take five index cards and put a self-care idea on each side. For example, one card may have Exercise (body) on one side and Read (mind) on the other. Another card features Journal (feelings) and Pray (spirit) on its respective sides. Yet another card has Play (kid) on one side and Rest (body) on the other. With all the answers from the Jeopardy Wheel written on a whiteboard in the five categories during the game, the group members can choose which ideas work best for them. Everyone puts their filled-out index cards in their bags.

I encourage children and adults to use their bags daily. Shake it up, pull out a card, look at each side, and pick one idea. Take fifteen minutes to simply care for yourself. Many, many participants have reported benefiting immensely from this simple activity through the years.

Private Time

He was so quiet, almost invisible, as he deftly blended into the group. He would isolate somewhat during free time, especially during unstructured play in the pool. I had to work very hard to get a smile from this ten-year-old, but once accomplished I could really feel a connection growing. Tommy always wanted to sit by me and tagged along as we made our way to different venues around the center. I could make him laugh when I acted silly, yet during group he kept himself under wraps.

Tommy intrigued me. What was going on inside this little guy? I consciously make it a point to know as little as possible about children during the first day of the process. Sure, I know about allergies, who is on medication, and who can't swim. All of that is essential. I want to start with a clean slate for each youngster and not become biased by what's reported on the family questionnaire. Later I learned that Tommy had lost his mom to the insidious disease of addiction. Shortly thereafter, Dad was arrested for a DUI with the kids in the car, so they were immediately placed in emergency foster care. Luckily, Tommy and his little sister were kept together so he could keep a watchful eye on her. This ten-year-old faced so many challenges at such a young age.

During the sharing exercise Tommy moved me in a powerful way. When it was his turn to share there was no anger, hurt, or disappointment in his words, looks, or actions. "I'm so proud of you, Dad. I knew how much you loved me by quickly doing all your tests, getting help, and getting us back. I love you, Dad." With tears filling his eyes he softly continued, "No more drugs, Dad. I need you." Honest sharing, real emotion, and great progress, but now it was time to talk about Mom. I had broached this subject near the end of the second day in the children's group only to be met by tears and Tommy quietly placing his face in his hands.

The simple mention of Mom brought both of them to tears. They had never talked about it since her death. I reflected that they both truly miss her a lot. Once Tommy indicated that she was in heaven I encouraged him to talk to her. This little guy closed his eyes and tilted his head slightly upward. "I miss you, Mommy," he began. "I still love you. I'll always love you." Tommy embraced his dad. His courageous act gave Dad permission to grieve as well. They hadn't talked about her simply because they didn't know how.

They went home that afternoon both emotionally drained. They had taken huge steps in their healing journey. It was Saturday night, and many friends were over to celebrate the weekend. Amidst all the laughter and love emanating through the house, Tommy found his dad and announced, "I need some private time." Dad later related to me that he thought his son had learned this in group, but we hadn't broached this subject yet. Tommy headed off to his room, and about ten minutes later Dad checked on him.

"What are you doing?" Dad inquired.

Tommy looked right at his dad and replied, "I'm talking to Mom."

They both had smiles on their faces.

Amanda Gets Safe

Unquestionably a diminutive eight-year-old dynamo, in many other respects Amanda was well beyond her years. Framed by blonde curls and green, almond-shaped eyes, her smile welcomed the world. Everyone wanted to be Amanda's friend. Giggles and muffled laughter accompanied her wherever she went. But this warm, carefree façade barely concealed a little girl challenged by her confusion, hurt, and fear. Amanda adored her mom more than anyone in the world yet suffered and struggled with her mother's steady descent into the abyss of alcoholism.

Her parents were separated, and Amanda lived with her father the majority of the time. He was an awesome parent, but despite his best efforts to shield Amanda, his youngest, from the chaos and insanity of her mom's illness, she and everyone else were entangled in it. Despite his concern, her dad accepted the deep bond Amanda had for her mother. Weekly, for almost six years, he drove her over an hour each way to participate in a children's program so she could better understand and successfully cope with the family's circumstances. A loving act. In exploring this extraordinary commitment he once remarked, "What I would have given had there been a program like this for me when I was a kid." His eyes filled with tears and he gave me a long heartfelt hug as he whispered, "Thanks for helping my daughter." He was giving his little one the gift he had been denied as a child: a safe place to grow, learn, and heal.

Amanda made great strides in the program. She quickly saw that she was not alone, that millions of other children love parents challenged by alcoholism and other drug addictions. She was relieved to understand that children don't make their parents drink and can't make them stop. These thoughts had really troubled her, often causing stomachaches and nightmares. Mom's drinking was not her fault. She became steadfast in her adherence to the basic program tenet: people with addictions are not bad people, though sometimes they do bad things. "My mom is full of goodness," she would share. "That mom plays with me, tucks me in bed at night, teaches me stuff, and tells me how special I am. I really love her." After a long sigh she continued, "I hate the mom who drinks. I would give anything to have my real mom back." Many heads nodded affirmatively. Her sentiments resonated with all.

One night, after an emotionally laden group session, Amanda hung around until we were all alone. "I must tell you something now. I can't hold it in any longer." We sat across from one another separated by a long, awkward silence. Finally she found the courage to explain what happened every other Saturday when she visited her mother. In the morning they would drive to her mom's favorite bar, where Amanda sat alone in the car waiting for Mom to return. As tears flowed she blurted out, "Sometimes Mom comes out in twenty minutes, sometimes longer." Then, sobbing, she declared, "Jerry, sometimes I wait till it gets dark outside. I pray for Mommy to come back, and I get so scared." I held this brave girl as she released emotions she'd buried deep inside for too long. Finally she continued, "Please don't take me away from my mom. I've never told anyone 'cause I'm scared I won't get to see her anymore. I love my mom."

I teach kids the importance of staying safe. They identify individuals, their "safe people," whom they can trust and call upon whenever they feel threatened or scared. Week after week we focused on these concepts with Amanda and the others. When Dad became aware of the circumstances he took many steps to protect his daughter, but legal proceedings often take lots of time. I made sure Amanda always carried a small plastic container that fit easily in her pocket with the names and phone numbers of her safe people, along with fifty cents. Both her dad and I reviewed various scenarios where it would be necessary for her to call a safe person.

Many weeks later, on a Saturday morning, Amanda waited in the car again for her mother to come out of the bar. "I started to panic, but then I remembered it's important to stay safe," she would later tell her group. She crossed a busy intersection at the crosswalk and found a pay phone.

There was no answer at her dad's, and she couldn't get through to her grandma. Finally, she heard her big brother's strong, reassuring voice, "I'll be there in ten minutes." Amanda recrossed the street and walked into the bar to search for the mom she adored.

Finding her at last, Amanda crawled into her mom's lap and hugged her ever so tightly. Amanda kissed her and said, "Billy is coming to get me right now. I love you, but I can't stay with you today. I just want to be a kid." Then, hopping to the floor she said, "I love you, Mommy. See you in two weeks." She navigated her way through the dimly lit bar and headed outside to find her big brother waiting.

CHAPTER FIVE

Let the Healing Begin

The Measure of a Man

L et's get an update on Judy, Angela, Brendan, and Evelyn, the family we've been following throughout this book. When Brent died tragically, Evelyn was only four years old. She is the baby in the family—Angela and Brendan's younger sister. The look on their faces when Mom gently and courageously told those three kids that their daddy had gone back home to be with God will always be etched in my memory.

Angela burst into tears, and Brendan quickly gasped for air. Shock immediately set in as the room filled with sobs and tears. Little Evelyn became wide-eyed and confused. I think she believed Daddy was just on a trip and would be back soon. Months later, Evelyn asked her mom, "Can we go to the daddy store and get a new daddy?"

Evelyn is a precious child with big, brown, innocent eyes and beautiful, long black hair. Every time I look at her, I see her dad. Sadly, she doesn't remember much about him. After her seventh birthday, it was her turn to go through the children's program. She was old enough to know the truth about her family, and I have no doubt that this would be exactly what her dad would want for her. She told anyone who would listen that it was now her turn to "have fun like Angela and Brendan got to do." Most of the time she was quiet and shy with a faint whisper for a voice, but that was about to change.

As hard as it was for me to believe, Angela was now a teenager and had blossomed into a beautiful and graceful young lady, still regularly attending the continuing-care night and in the Alateen program. Life was good for Angela, but there had been plenty of struggles along the way. It was difficult to work through her feelings of guilt about her father's death. She had been going on the trip with her dad the night he died, until he changed his mind at the last minute. "If only I had been with him, he'd still be alive," she once shared in an individual session. "He wouldn't have been drinking if I were in the car." Today, people who love her surround her, and she realizes that she's not alone. She has truly accepted that her dad's death is not her fault. And you should see her dance! It's simply breathtaking to watch the joy and grace she exudes in each performance.

Brendan is a good big brother. While he tries his best to hide it from the world at times, he's a very gentle and sensitive kid who misses the loving presence of his father in his life. Worn out from dealing with his dad's death, he had taken a break from continuing care. Even though it was always Brendan's decision to talk in group or not, the program brought up so many memories of Dad—good times, stress, relapse, conflict, love, anger, helplessness, and death—that he needed the space. It was an important milestone that he could communicate this to me and set a boundary for himself. It was huge that he was coming back to support his little sister when it was Evelyn's turn to join the children's program. That's the kind of young man he is.

Although everyone on staff registers children and families for the program, only two or three of us facilitate each experience, so we don't always realize what common themes exist until kid introductions at our first session. Chills ran down my spine and my eyes teared up as I learned that three other kids in this group, besides Brendan and Evelyn, had lost a parent to this disease. Although that was a first in all my professional years working with groups, I have never doubted the existence of a Higher Power in my work. I always feel this loving presence in each group of kids and parents who come for healing. Whether the name is God, Creator, Buddha, or whatever, the Higher Power is always right there in the group.

Malcolm started to cry as he shared his picture with us. "I miss my dad," he began. The room got utterly still and quiet. "I'd give up anything for just one more day with him. Just one more day." The pent-up words rushed out, "No one understands."

"I understand." It was Brendan. He simply got out of his chair, walked over to Malcolm, and put his hand on Malcolm's shoulder. "I know what it's like. I miss my dad, too, and I hate addiction." Malcolm stood, they hugged one another, and both cried. Gradually, everyone shared their feelings and offered support and encouragement to each other. Evelyn was last. Tears were streaming down her face, yet her voice was both stronger and louder. "I miss my daddy, too." That's all she could say at that point, but what a powerful moment for Malcolm, Brendan, and Evelyn. Everyone's heart in that circle was deeply touched.

I had enjoyed a good connection with Brent. I deeply respected and admired the love he had for his family. He was a good man who wanted a better life for his children than what he had experienced as a child. He kept picking himself up after each relapse and fought the disease valiantly until he ultimately succumbed to it. Many parents avoid me after a slip, but he kept bringing his kids back and working on a better life. I so wanted Evelyn to know more about him.

After completing the program with Mom and Brendan, Evelyn and I sat alone. I let her know that her daddy had been my friend and I had liked him a lot. She interrupted me right in the middle of my discourse and blurted out, "Was he a good man?"

I looked into those big brown eyes and emphatically replied, "Your father was a very good man. He loved you, Mommy, Angela, and Brendan with all his heart." She smiled. "Addiction trapped him and took him away, but he was still a really good person." Evelyn shook her head and cried just a little. That was the only question she asked. Now she knows the answer.

You're It!

W hen children really understand that addiction is not their fault, a huge burden is lifted from their shoulders and a newfound lightness envelops their hearts and spirit. This is deepened simply by being with other boys and girls who have been going through the same ordeal. They finally have peers they can talk to, cry with, and support in the healing process. For them to realize they are not alone only adds to the hope awakening inside of them. As they are gently encouraged by staff and peers, these courageous children talk, trust, and feel in brand-new ways. They discuss their problems and let out a variety of feelings that they've been holding onto for a very long time. Some even tell secrets they thought they would never share. As these rocks come out of the bag, children feel incredible relief.

All along the way we play with them. What a gift to watch their play become more spontaneous and free as the healing process unfolds! We enjoy many moments of laughter and silliness on this journey. The more serious and adultlike the group, the more the staff gets silly and creates opportunities to laugh and have fun. We teach and model when it's time for play and when it's time for serious activities, as many have never learned to distinguish the two. I can tell it's working when kids come back in the morning with smiles on their faces and a joke or funny story to share. Making friends, having fun, and glowing in a safe, child-centered environment, these boys and girls are becoming children—some for the first time in their lives.

In working with their parents, grandparents, and guardians, I always encourage them to set a weekly play date individually with each child. The purpose is to connect and have fun. It's about spending time together.

Out of the Mouths of Babes

It was early Saturday morning—a rare weekend off. I was heading home to celebrate Dad's birthday. As I settled into my seat it was still dark outside. I closed my eyes and drifted off to sleep, waking occasionally as a bag bumped against the seat or someone slammed shut an overhead bin.

Suddenly I heard a distinctive, familiar voice. It had to be Reggie. He and his three siblings had been through the Betty Ford Center Children's Program a couple of times and were regulars at the Wednesday evening continuing-care program. The whole family worked hard to overcome Dad's and Mom's addiction to alcohol and other drugs. Along the way there had been many setbacks, pitfalls, and disappointments, but they never gave up. Though I cared deeply about each member of this family, Reggie had stolen my heart. The youngest, he was friendly and outspoken, greeting the world with love and joy. Though he joked, giggled, and laughed most of the time, Reggie occasionally stopped people in their tracks by speaking the truth with the terseness of a true warrior.

I opened my eyes to see the whole family awkwardly negotiating the aisle with way too much carry-on baggage. It was 6:30 AM on a day off—way too early for this!

I instinctively reached for my newspaper and opened it wide to conceal my identity. Children freak out when we meet unexpectedly away from work. "What are you doing here?" they may blurt out in disbelief. Many assume that I just live at the Center and patiently wait for them to return to group, answer their phone calls during times of trouble, or quickly respond to their e-mails. That day I felt incapable of interacting without at least one cup of coffee in my system.

They settled in two rows ahead of me. What a gift to hear their banter and discourse throughout the hour-long flight! As the plane pulled up to the Jetway in San Francisco I truly thought I had escaped. Little did I realize that the plane being only half full would give me away. When the bell signaled our safe arrival, Reggie, forgetting his backpack underneath the seat, bolted toward the door. As he came back to retrieve it, he saw me and shrieked loudly, "Jerry!"

He moved with the speed, force, and purpose of an Olympic sprinter. Other passengers were swept aside as he made his way back and jumped into my arms—it looked like he was parting the Red Sea. There was a collective sigh from everyone, almost a Hallmark moment.

Reggie turned around to face everyone in front of him and proudly declared, "He's my therapist." He briefly turned toward me with a mischievous look in his eye, then whirled back around declaring, "He keeps teaching me it's not my fault." As he finally headed off the plane he flashed me a huge smile and giggled one more time.

The Bright Side of Addiction

A s children grow and heal, their perspective changes about a lot of things. Many benefit immensely from the alcoholic/addict getting help and the whole family working on treatment and recovery, individually and collectively. New relationships emerge in the family, and fun, love, kindness, caring, and joy slowly become present in a brand-new way. While things are far from perfect and challenges present themselves around every corner, youngsters are deeply grateful for the positive changes. They somehow seem to appreciate these gifts more and cherish them. They enjoy all the new friends they've made, the tools they've developed, and the strengths they've honed as they contend with this insidious disease. Many are proud of their resilience and are eager to share it with others.

For children I've worked with whose parents have been in recovery for all of the kids' lives, the dynamic is different. Many had no clue about the family addiction problem, as their parents were not sure about when and how to tell their little ones. These children, upon hearing, learning, and understanding the true nature of addiction, typically have a newfound pride, respect, and admiration for their recovering parents. They are grateful for all their parents' hard work and recovery.

It's fascinating to watch kids see the bright side even if their loved one remains stuck in the disease. They are relieved to realize it's not their fault and come to accept they can't make it better. While the latter can be difficult to remember each day, it does provide relief. These boys and girls take comfort in a new support system they can call upon at any time. They gradually develop a greater understanding of themselves and their families. Many develop a closer connection to a Higher Power and engage in spiritual practices: prayer, quiet time, and helping others. They are comforted in remembering they are not alone, and they hold hope close to their hearts—hope for a better today and a brighter tomorrow.

A Simple Gratitude

Julie was very quiet and detached. A pervasive sadness enveloped her and set her apart from the others. I was intrigued by what issues had this eleven-year-old so preoccupied and glum. It didn't take long for this picture to become clear. About forty-five minutes into the program we go around the circle and I ask each participant a variety of questions such as favorite color, a food you hate, a vacation place you'd like to visit, and what job you'd like when you grow up. If the mood feels right I conclude this exercise with, "If you had one wish to make things better for your family, what would you wish for?" The children's responses were all over the place—some poignant, others outrageous—yet all very honest. Julie shared, "I wish we had a little more money." I was touched by the simplicity of her wish and the pain in her voice. Many kids wish for a mansion or $10 million, or an expensive sports car, but not just a little money.

During our walk around the center, Julie's eyes got real big when we visited the cafeteria. She excitedly asked one of the counselors, "Are you sure we can get whatever we want and eat as much as we'd like?" When she heard the affirmative response, she couldn't stop a huge grin from filling her face. I'll never forget that Julie made it a ritual to thank the staff profusely after every lunch and snack. She was so grateful for all the good food each and every day.

When it came to money, Julie lived in a very poor family. While Dad was active in his disease she often lived with Grandma, when Dad allowed it. Other times she and Dad would stay at friends' houses, but sometimes they lived out of their car. Julie had been through the program before with Grandma while Dad was still hooked on drugs. Within six months a miracle happened: Dad sought out and wholeheartedly embraced recovery. All too often, many programs just help the alcoholic/addict first and then offer support to the family. Maybe if we started with the children and families first, more addicted people would ultimately seek help as their loved ones refused to support the disease anymore.

I was very excited that Julie would be coming back to the program with her dad. This was another opportunity to treat her with the same gentle kindness and caring she'd experienced before. Something was really different this time, though. There was a light in her eyes that I'd never seen before. She was ecstatic that her daddy had found recovery. Money was still a huge challenge for this family, but there was a new sense of hope in the air. Dad had a new job, and an apartment soon followed. Julie was an integral part of group this time around, as she spontaneously played and connected with the others in a whole new way.

Her sharing with Dad was both poignant and powerful. The counselor asked Julie at the conclusion of the exercise just how much she hated addiction for messing up her family. This eleven-year-old thoughtfully pondered the question and replied, "Not anymore." Then Julie looked directly into her dad's eyes and continued, "If it wasn't for addiction, me and you would never have made it here. Look at all the great friends we've met, Dad. Even if I could go back and change things I wouldn't." Her eyes slowly filled with tears as she concluded, "I wouldn't change a thing because you're the best dad that anybody could ever have."

When it came to their relationship, Julie and her dad, both now growing in healthy ways, were blessed with a multitude of riches. Even though she was only eleven, Julie embraced this with all her heart.

~&

Facing Challenges

Challenges are part of everyday life. They come in all sizes and shapes. For all these children the issue of addiction is never far away. Many wonder if their loved ones will ever stop drinking or using other drugs. Will they ever make it to get help? Will the family tear apart? For those youngsters with a loved one in recovery, the challenges are both different and similar. Will they stop doing T&R? Will the alcoholic/addict relapse? They also wonder if the family will tear apart. These thoughts are a constant in their lives. Add to that the challenges of making friends, fitting in, doing well in school, and just being themselves.

For years I've introduced kids to the concept of safe people, adults in their lives they can turn to for support and guidance. The research on resilience points to the presence of a caring, nurturing adult in one's life as a key factor in overcoming hardship and adversity in healthy, balanced ways. For lots of youngsters the relationship they develop with their group facilitator is their first such experience. Kids delight and relish in such a relationship, and many have been so emotionally hungry for this they simply can't get enough. From the moment I meet children I'm steadily becoming a bridge for them to hook up with other safe people in their lives, perhaps a recovering parent, relative, teacher, counselor, coach, neighbor, or minister. This task is easier to complete for the boys and girls I see in continuing care because there's more time to accomplish it, while a four- or five-day program makes it more challenging for me.

I remain a safe person, as does the entire staff, for as long as kids want. I promise to be here for them, and I am. They get the 800 number they can call 24/7, an e-mail address, a snail-mail address. I return every call, shoot back an e-mail, return a letter for every one I receive. Kids know if they send me a funny drawing, I'll send an even funnier one back. Kids get in touch when times get tough, but also when milestones and good things happen to them.

I've been invited to so many games, birthday parties, bar and bat mitzvahs, graduations, weddings, baby showers, and the like. About once a month an adult I worked with years ago will call to say, "Thanks." It's always such a thrill. When these kids have safe people in their lives, it helps them to meet their daily challenges.

A Good Separation

Buddy has already faced many daunting challenges in his life. His dad has been in prison since Buddy was two years old. Mom has been in and out of his life since the beginning, as the allure of methamphetamines and alcohol keep taking her away. This eleven-year-old is so blessed in that the one constant in his life has been a kind, caring, and loving aunt who's really been his mother. For the past nine years she has been gently guiding, shaping, and protecting this precious boy. She made sure he got to the program and had a chance to grow, play, learn, and heal.

Buddy stayed very quiet throughout the entire process. He took virtually everything in and remained engaged at all times yet preferred to stay in the background. If you asked him a question he'd offer a thoughtful reply that added depth and meaning to the discussion. Buddy simply wouldn't initiate the conversation, so I had to make sure he didn't just blend in or stay on the sidelines with each building activity.

This is pretty much how it stayed over all five days. I had to constantly remind myself not to forget about him and purposefully include him in each phase of the process. He came in each day with a smile on his face and was ready for the adventure that was about to unfold. Buddy did everything well yet never directed any attention to himself. That's just not Buddy.

At graduation I noticed he had to wipe away some tears when it was time to say good-bye. He hugged the entire staff and went up to each of his peers and said, "Thank you." That's all he said. As I observed this I couldn't help but wonder what he meant by that— thanks for playing with me, thanks for being a friend, thanks for helping me know that I'm not alone—maybe all the above. It would be over fourteen months until I heard from Buddy again. Little did I realize how much he had learned in the program and held so closely to his heart.

I was on my way to speak at a prevention conference across the country. As I disembarked from a long and weary flight, the first voice-mail message was an emergency call from Buddy. He didn't sound panicked and stressed out as most youngsters do when they call about an emergency. It was good to hear his voice, but I wondered what was going on. I left two messages, one from the airport and another as I arrived at the hotel. I hadn't been in my hotel room for more than ten minutes when he called. Upon hearing my voice, his was now full of emotions. He spoke quickly as the words kept pouring out of his mouth. He kept repeating, "Jerry, you are going to be real proud of me," until I told him to stop, take a deep breath, and slow down. He indicated that his mom was very ill. She was in intensive care because her liver wasn't working anymore. When his aunt told him this, he begged and pleaded to go visit his mom, yet Aunt Teddy said this wasn't a good idea.

Buddy wouldn't let up on his request. Apparently with tears he approached his aunt one more time. "I need to see my mom," he pleaded. "I promise to leave her disease outside the door." These simple yet powerful words stopped Teddy in her tracks. She thought Buddy would be overwhelmed by the ICU and the progressively failing condition of her sister. Tears welled up in my eyes as Buddy really got the essence of the children's program: separating a loved one from the disease and talking openly and honestly about your feelings. Aunt Teddy finally relented.

Buddy told me that he stood right next to his mom even though she was sleeping. He related there were lots of tubes, monitors, and nurses everywhere. Buddy kissed his mom on the forehead and softly told her, "I love you, Mommy. I'll always love you. You are a good person. Don't forget." He told me that a smile appeared on her face when he told her that. Buddy shared that he was feeling sad but glad that he got to see his mother.

At the end of our conversation Buddy asked if I was proud of him. "Absolutely," I replied, only to be met by lots of giggling on the other end of the phone. Buddy, thank you. I'm so full of pride, joy, and gratitude—much more than you'll ever know.

Being There for Others

T hrough the years in children's programs, I have personally witnessed many friendships forged that have endured the tests of time. I can't emphasize enough the power of youngsters truly understanding that they are not alone. Through group they come to meet other kids who've walked similar paths and really understand. Beyond the silence, secrecy, stigma, and shame, they get introduced to new "brothers" and "sisters." Many stand tall in helping one another, both during the group and outside of it as well. I've been to more funerals for these children's parents than I'd ever care to remember. Some people just take their active addiction to the grave. So many youngsters show up to comfort and support the kids who've lost their loved ones to the disease. It's their simple yet honest words, a gentle touch on the shoulder, and a heartfelt hug that can make such a difference to a grieving child. I've watched the power of this repeatedly.

As children appreciate the gift of getting help, many want to pay it forward. Their courage and strength overwhelm me as they choose to tell their story to others. It's not just the kids whose families are in recovery who take a stand. Some kids living with active addiction also take a stand, as well as children whose loved ones have died. They share their message at school and in their communities. I'm always encouraging children to really think this through before taking such a big step and to discuss this thoroughly with their families. Those who step forward break the silence and find their voice, a strong and powerful one. A question I routinely ask each of them is "Why?" Here's the typical response, "If I can help one other kid, then it's worth it." It's such a noble act of giving back.

Time for Change

Mikey walked in with a huge smile on his face. Somehow he knew right from the beginning that he was in a good place, a safe place. This eight-year-old was equal parts funny, sincere, and extraordinarily kind to others. He was a master storyteller as he captivated kids and adults alike with entertaining stories and hilarious anecdotes. Underneath all these amazing gifts lurked plenty of pain and sadness, often manifested through nasty stomachaches. We saw more and more glimpses of this emotional residue as the program unfolded.

The primary issue that Mikey had been struggling with was his parents' divorce. While Dad's drug addiction troubled him, it was clearly not getting to live with both his parents that hurt the most. Mikey soaked in all the program offerings like a dry sponge. He gained much relief in learning how to separate the addiction from the father he adored. Through his artwork, story, and verbal communication he reiterated time and again, "Even though my daddy is trapped, I still love him anyway and I know he loves me." His eyes would well up when he made this declaration. When Mom also participated on the final two days there was lots of honesty and healing for them during the process. They had grown closer, made a plan for self-care, and found a real sense of hope along the way.

A few weeks after the program, the staff received this letter from Mikey and his mother.

I wanted to share this story with you. The other night we were driving home and Mikey said to me, "Mom, thank you for protecting me from the addiction." I told him that that was my job and that I would always do my best to protect him. Later that night when we were getting ready for bed, I asked him if he had remembered what he said to me in the car. He said yes. I asked him if he had learned a little from the program. His eyes got wide and he told me, "Mom, I didn't learn a little, I learned a LOT!"

Thank you from the bottom of my heart for your graciousness and dedication. All of the children who attended the kids' program really need you and I know they benefited from being there. Mikey learned so much and truly seemed so much lighter after that first day. Things just seemed to click for him. He couldn't wait to tell his teacher and school counselor about the weekend. They were so excited for him. He has talked to his dad a little bit, and although his main concern is Dad "doing drugs," his father has assured him he hasn't used anything for a long time.

I appreciate all of you. Your kindness showed from the very first moment we met you. Again, thank you for everything and for truly making a difference in our lives. The program was a great gift to all of us. You are all a great blessing.

What a gift for the staff to receive such a letter! Here it was for all of us to savor and enjoy.

Last week Mikey and his mom walked into the program offices unannounced. Staff came scurrying from all directions, as it's always a major event when a child comes back to visit. There was that big grin prominently featured on Mikey's angelic face. Mom broke the ice by stating, "Mikey has something to give you." He started giggling as he struggled to hold the giant butter container he was carrying.

"Since the program," Mom continued, "Mikey has been collecting and saving pennies so another little kid could come here."

Mikey proudly gave the heavy tub to his counselor. "Thank you for helping me so much. This will give someone else a chance. I would do anything to help another boy or girl not to have to hurt anymore. Help some people, poor people, to get to come here." Never have we all felt so rich in the children's program. Another harvest right before our eyes!

~❧~

Pass It On

Annie has many, many strengths. This eleven-year-old has a huge heart, deeply rooted passion and a genuine love for others that go way beyond her years. Her father's continuing struggle with addiction still hurts her deeply at times, yet the children's program has helped her face this difficult challenge in a healthy, balanced way. During our time together all the staff took turns holding up a "mirror" to Annie, as we do with each youngster, to reflect her strengths, gifts, and special qualities she's been blessed with to live life to the fullest. She learned important information and developed new skills along the way to help in this regard. Annie more fully realized that she had the love and support of a caring mom and awesome siblings to guide her in good times and tough ones as well.

Some of the seeds we plant in the children's program take hold immediately; some lay dormant for a while; and others wash away. We are farmers who keep on throwing lots of seeds, lots of seeds. Slowly and gradually a harvest was about to bloom right before my eyes. Saying good-bye to Annie and her family was very difficult, as they had all touched my heart. I had been captivated by Annie's spirit and the caring way she viewed the world. When the hope for healing was dimmed by the huge shadow addiction cast on this family, Annie reached out via e-mail. Staff promise each child always to be available if kids ever need help. I'll never forget my last words to Annie, "I'm really proud of you. Keep in touch." Big hearts can easily be hurt and broken, which happened to Annie again and again. She conveyed this with a paucity of words: "Dad relapsed. What can I do? It hurts and I'm scared." I kept in touch and continued to reinforce all the major messages in the program: not your fault, not alone, reach out to safe people, addiction is a disease, care for yourself. I pray daily for each child and family I've ever been blessed to serve. When they reach out, I'll be there to listen, validate, encourage, educate, and empower.

A few months ago Annie e-mailed me and wanted to interview me for a school report. I gladly replied but really didn't understand the significance of her assignment. For her social studies class she was writing an essay about an Everyday Hero. I was deeply honored that Annie chose to write about me, yet I was even more moved that she would go public about her family problem with all her classmates. Addiction is characterized by silence, secrecy, shame, and stigma, and here was this courageous eleven-year-old breaking the silence and speaking her truth. She wanted to pass along all she learned to others in need.

Jerry Moe

Jerry Moe was born in San Francisco on June 30, 1955. Jerry Moe is the national director of the children's program at Betty Ford Center in California. The Betty Ford Center is a place where addicts go to get help. I have been to the Betty Ford Center Children's Program with Jerry. He taught me a lot about addiction. Learning about addiction is important so kids of all ages can learn what happens inside an addict's body. He also teaches kids not to do drugs and the impact addiction has on the rest of your family.

Jerry taught me that addiction is a type of brain disease. Addiction takes over the person's body, and addiction is in control. You can get rid of addiction with treatment and recovery, which Jerry calls T&R. Nobody except an addict can fix the problem. An addict has to ask for help before he will become sober. The addict's family has to take care of themselves, not the addict. Jerry teaches kids that their parents' addiction isn't the kid's fault, and it isn't the kid's job to fix their parents' problems.

Jerry is my hero because I know that I can trust him with my feelings and I know that he will do everything in his power to help me. He is very good at making people laugh even when they are going through a really rough time in their life.

I think that the whole world should try to be as understanding and compassionate as Jerry is. After going through the program with Jerry, I think that it will be easier to say no when people offer me drugs or alcohol because he has taught me so much and I have actually lived through what addiction does to a family.

Soon thereafter she needed to prepare a speech for her public speaking class. It had to be about something she was truly passionate about. Annie wanted to tell the truth about addiction—this time to the whole school! There was a long and lengthy family discussion about this, as doing so impacted Annie's siblings as well. They talked and shared feelings; each spoke their truth and came to a compromise that supported everyone. Annie, with a clear and strong conviction, was moving forward because "If I can help one other kid like I've been helped, it's all worth it."

Addiction

My passion is teaching kids and adults about addiction. "Knowledge is like white blood cells." White blood cells fight off diseases. Knowing about addiction is like a white blood cell because knowing what addiction does to your body and to your family will help people decide never to try drugs or alcohol. I would like to share what I have learned about addiction, hoping that you will take this to heart.

Addiction is a type of brain disease. It can also be explained like an allergy. Like I can eat strawberries and I am fine, but when my sister eats strawberries she has an allergic reaction. Some people can have alcohol and not be addicted, like my mom, and some people become addicts, like my dad. He can't help it because he has a brain disease. This is where your knowledge fights off the disease.

Getting rid of addiction isn't the easiest thing to do. You need treatment and recovery. Treatment is going through at least a thirty-day program at a facility. Recovery is when you are working your program and staying sober. That means going to meetings and stuff like that. The only person who can get rid of addiction is the addict. The addict has to want to fix it before it will work.

When anybody you know is addicted to drugs or alcohol, you will have feelings that you can't really explain. You may feel hurt, scared, worried, upset, nervous, sad, and other things. Don't think that you are the only one that feels this way because you aren't. Many kids and adults feel these feelings everyday. These feelings are one hundred percent normal. I feel all of these feelings every day, but I know that I'm probably going to feel these things the rest of my life and I'm okay with that. I have to accept the way I feel and move on with my life. I'm not going to sit around and watch life pass me by. I am going to live my life to the fullest.

The addict's family has to take care of themselves, not the addict. To all of the kids that have parents with addiction, IT ISN'T YOUR FAULT AND ISN'T YOUR JOB TO FIX! I know it might seem like it is your fault but it really isn't, and it most certainly isn't your job to fix. You need to live your life the way you want. You are in control of your life, and don't make the choice to try drugs or alcohol because it isn't fair to yourself and to those who really care about you.

In the program you learn the serenity prayer. This is how it goes. God grant me the serenity to accept the things I cannot change, the courage to change the things I can, and the wisdom to know the difference.

Teaching kids and adults about addiction is my passion and

I am pleased with myself and that's the way it should be.
Annie, you are my hero . . . yesterday, today, every day.

❧

Final Words

It was near the end of another successful children's program. In their small groups the kids and the grown-ups had just verbally exchanged "What I Like and Love About You" cards with their family members. We would never want to end a program without talking about all the good stuff, specifically all the special qualities that endear us to our loved ones. This is always such a touching experience.

At the conclusion of this exercise the counselor asked if anyone had anything they'd like to share with the small group before heading off to graduation. Letti, age seven, quickly raised her hand, which was quite surprising as she was the quietest participant of all. This brave child had made many, many positive strides in the program despite all the difficult challenges she's endured in her young life. Referred by Children's Protective Services to our program, Letti had been horrendously abused and exhibited poor social skills. She had been blossoming here, so there was real hope that with a solid continuing-care plan she could continue to find her strengths and resilience. Letti looked right at Cindy and declared, "I am glad you were here. Thanks for being my friend." Cindy, also a CPS referral who's been through way more than any youngster should ever have to contend with, immediately replied,

"You made it easier for me to be here." They spontaneously got up from their chairs, met in the middle, and gave each other a hug. What a moment!

Before anyone could even compose themselves, Tassa raised her hand next. This ten-year-old also had been quiet and reserved over the four days. Incredibly kind to all the others, she had only shown emotion when we played the Addiction game. Tassa got in touch with deep sadness about losing her mom to the disease and simply cried for a long time after sharing with the group. Afterward she looked relieved and much lighter, yet she soon became quiet and reserved all over again. What in the world could be coming next? Once called upon, Tassa stood up and went right to the center of the circle. She then slowly revolved around the group, stopping for a few seconds and nodding gratefully to each of her peers in friendly acknowledgment. When everyone had been singled out in this unique way, Tassa proudly declared, "I want you to know that I never could have done this without you all here to help me." Everyone cried.

I am not always exactly sure how much children get from a program. That day I was blessed with clear evidence of what three special kids had received. I stand in awe and wonder simply to be part of their process.

Games and Activities

Addiction

Bicycle

(Ages four and up)

This exercise provides a hands-on experiential process that not only captures children's imagination but also focuses on the reality of addiction. Children see and feel how the bicycle ride symbolizes addiction with a loss of control. They gain an understanding of this disease and have fun doing it.

Description

"Okay kids, we are going to take a ride on our octocycle!" (assuming there are eight kids and eight chairs). Each child represents a family member, with the alcoholic/addict steering at the front. An invisible bar connects each seat to emphasize the rigidness and enmeshment of the disease. Children sit in their chairs and make the circular motion of bicycle pedals with their arms and hands.

By reading a story (see "Bicycle Ride Narrative" on page 143) the facilitator "takes the children for a ride." An initially peaceful, joyful journey gradually turns into a rainstorm on a steep downhill grade. Suddenly, no brakes! Crash!

After the crash ask the children the following questions:

1. How did you feel throughout the bike ride? Some comments have been: "Scary." "I felt out of control." Another child certainly drawn to crisis and drama stated, "Exciting."
2. How was that like living in an alcoholic home?
3. Could you see how the disease progresses?
4. Was it your fault? "No, it's not your fault."
5. Where can you go to get help?
6. If the alcoholic gets back on the bike, does that mean you have to? Each time this is asked a chorus of "no's" echoes loudly.

Example

See the questions above. Nine-year-old Danielle summed it up best. "The bike ride was fun at first but scary at the end. Alcoholics don't have brakes when it comes to drinking. I guess relapse is when they think they have brakes even though they don't."

Affirmations

• "You can get help."
• "You can make helpful choices to stay safe."

- "It's not your fault; you don't have to be alone anymore."

Comments

- The exercise also helps children bring the disease to conscious reality by talking about feelings.
- Learning the disease is not their fault and brainstorming ways of taking care of themselves are made possible by this game.

Materials

- Bicycle Ride Narrative
- Chairs

Bicycle Ride Narrative

"Okay, everybody in position.

"We are going for a nice ride through the country. It's a beautiful day. The sun is out and the birds are chirping. There's no wind, just a gentle breeze. We are pedaling slowly, breathing evenly, enjoying the scenery, and laughing with each other. We put on the brakes slowly as a dog wags his way across our path.

"As we are gathering speed, a few dark clouds begin to appear over the horizon and the breeze becomes a little more stiff as the smooth pavement turns into a dirt road. We begin to pedal a little harder and grab onto the handlebars a little tighter. The clouds are becoming darker, and some light rain begins to fall as the dirt road is getting slippery and bumpy. We keep putting on the brakes while still moving. We have to lean forward and pedal harder as we are going up a hill. Our legs and stomach are sore as our hands grab the handlebars even tighter. The rain is coming down harder, and at times the bike almost tips over.

"We reach the top of the hill exhausted, but it is raining so hard we have to keep moving. We start pedaling faster as we go down the other side of the hill. The rain is slapping harder onto our faces. The bike is sliding back and forth across the road. Loud sounds of thunder can be heard. Lightning strikes a tree near us. We are pedaling faster and faster, and holding on tighter and tighter. Our feet keep slipping off the pedals as we go faster and faster. Skipping and sliding, we try the brakes. The brakes don't hold—they no longer work. We're losing control! Pedals are spinning faster and faster. The road is much steeper and bumpier as we go faster and faster, trying the brakes (no brakes) and holding on for dear life. CRASH—the bike tips over."

Bicycle Questions

1. What was that like for you?
2. How was this like alcoholism/addiction?
3. How was this like what you experience in your own home?
4. Was everyone affected?
5. When you fell down, who did you have to help first?
6. What would you do if the alcoholic addict wanted to get back on the bike and continue down the hill?
7. Whose fault is it?
8. Where can you go to get help?

"Okay, since your family cycle is all busted up we have a new cycle for each of you."

The Addiction Game
(Ages six and up)

Using both a visual and kinesthetic format, the Addiction Game enables youngsters to differentiate between the person they love and care about and the disease that consumes and overtakes that person. An extremely powerful exercise, it demonstrates that addiction is not the children's fault and that they are powerless to make it better.

Description

The group facilitator asks for a child to role-play the dependent person. The facilitator role-plays the disease of addiction. Starting with alcohol and other drugs, the disease makes all kinds of promises to the dependent if only that person would drink or use a little, "I'll make all your problems go away. I'll get rid of all your uncomfortable feelings. I'll make you more popular, funny, strong, and better looking." The dependent gradually gives in and begins using the chemicals. At first it appears that the disease really is becoming a good friend to the dependent.

After a short while the disease sneaks up on the dependent and quickly grabs him or her by the arms. Despite repeated struggling and pleading, the person is hooked and the disease simply won't let go. A discussion ensues about how the disease is now totally in charge of the person's life. The group talks about how none of the promises ever come true, how the person is trapped, and how problems and uncomfortable feelings accumulate instead of going away. The dependent shares how he or she feels to be so stuck. Typical responses range from scared and hopeless to angry and totally helpless.

An option here is to invite other children to try to free the "stuck family member." Youngsters struggle physically, beg and plead, make empty threats, and try all sorts of means to get the dependent unstuck, all to no avail. Through this added activity children understand that the addiction is not their fault and they can't make it better. Perhaps for the first time youngsters can separate the person they love from the disease they've come to despise and hate.

Example

Emily harbored intense anger and sadness over her mother's recent relapse. By playing the dependent she quickly experienced how helpless her mother became and how the disease totally ran her life. "I really understand how sick my mom becomes. She's out of control." With tears streaming down her face, Emily stammered, "I love my mom but I'm still mad at her for getting sick again. But I really hate this disease. It takes Mom away. I really hate it." Somehow this activity helped Emily to realize the difference between her mom and her mom's addiction.

Affirmations

"It's not my fault. I can't make it better."

"I'm not alone. Lots of kids deal with this problem daily."

"All my feelings are okay."

Comments

- Repeat this exercise until all the youngsters have had an opportunity to kinesthetically experience how it feels to be addicted.
- Use other substances or processes for youngsters to get hooked on—cigarettes, food, gambling, work, and relationships all can be stressed here.

Letters to the Disease

(Ages seven and up)

An excellent follow-up to the Addiction Game, this exercise allows youngsters to express deep-seated feelings about the disease that has created many of their families' problems. Writing a letter facilitates the process of helping children realize their powerlessness over family addiction. It also provides a way for kids to begin their own recovery by taking good care of themselves.

Descriptions

Based on the graphic illustrations of the Addiction Game (where youngsters can clearly differentiate between their loved ones and the disease that consumes them), this activity begins when the facilitator gives each group member a piece of paper with the words "Dear Addiction" at the top of the page. The facilitator instructs the children to write a letter to the disease, reassuring them that no one outside the group will ever see these letters. After helping them find a comfortable spot, the facilitator roams around the room and offers support and encouragement as they complete this task.

Children quite often express anger, hurt, sadness, fear, guilt, and shame. They describe the problems that have overwhelmed their loved ones, as well as their families. The group facilitator may give the youngsters the option of sharing their letters with the group if they so desire. After taking a day to discuss the letters and the feelings that developed as a result of them, the group can symbolically burn or bury these letters to let their feelings go.

Example

Dylan, a shy and withdrawn twelve-year-old, approached his letter writing with unusual vigor. He unfurled a barrage of anger at the disease that stuck his parents. Dylan also expressed fear that it could happen to him, "I am scared this nightmare might happen to me when I grow up. I don't want it to, but I'm scared it will trap me too." At this point Dylan quietly cried tears he had been storing for quite some time. He received much love and support from the group as he released these pent-up feelings.

Affirmations

"All my feelings are okay."

"I can express my feelings honestly, even my anger and fear."

"The disease is not my fault."

"My parents really do love me, but they are ill and might not always be able to show it."

Comments

- Help younger children write their letters by providing some assistance with general ideas and spelling.
- Even if children choose not to read their letters to the group, a general discussion of the feelings that surfaced during the writing brings children relief in knowing they are not alone in their family problems and feelings.
- Help youngsters make the connection between sharing feelings and then letting go of them by burning or burying their

letters. This assists them in understanding they can share anger without hurting themselves or others.

Materials

- "Dear Addiction" worksheets
- Pencils

Bubble Gum Family

(Ages six and up)

In a simple yet powerful way, Bubble Gum Family helps children understand what happens to everyone in a family struggling with addiction. Frequently used as a demonstration during community education sessions on how to work with young children of addiction, this activity helps children of all ages learn and have fun in the process.

Description

Almost everyone has had some experience chewing bubble gum. Remember how sticky it becomes after a few quick chews if you take it out of your mouth? Yuck! Have you ever had a big wad of gum stuck on the bottom of your shoe?

In this game everyone imagines there are 9,997 pieces of slightly chewed bubble gum in an imaginary circle on the floor. Children volunteer to role-play an addicted parent, the spouse, and several children. Using a narrative, the facilitator orchestrates a scenario in which everyone in the family gets stuck in the addiction (bubble gum).

First the addicted parent gets stuck by using alcohol and other drugs. The spouse and children get stuck in their attempts to help the addicted parent. Once stuck in the gum everyone has a hard time moving. They lose choice in what they think and do. Only by first taking good care of themselves can family members get unstuck. Different strategies for taking good care of oneself and the progression of the disease are stressed.

Example

This activity allowed Brian, age twelve, to understand how he impedes his mother's recovery by constantly taking care of her. Brian and three others played the roles of his father and siblings. Brian's mom was stuck in the center, and the rest of the family got stuck trying to help her. We instructed Brian and the others to circle very closely around his mom. Then we asked Mom to come out of the bubble gum. Brian said, "Even if she wanted to, she couldn't move because everyone else is in the way trying to take care of her. Boy, I guess it's true that if I take care of me, I give Mom the space to do the same for herself. I think I understand it now but it's hard to let go of her. I guess it begins with me."

Affirmations

- "I can trust my feelings to help me know what's best."

Comments

- Allow children the opportunity to role-play various family members, which lets them see how everyone becomes stuck in similar ways.
- Process feelings and discuss how this exercise is similar to the children's family experiences.

Material

- Bubble Gum Family Narrative

Bubble Gum Family Narrative

"We're going to do an activity now called Bubble Gum Family. Almost everyone has chewed bubble gum. There are all different kinds of bubble gum: Hubba Bubba, Carefree, Bazooka, or Bubble Yum Bubble Gum are just a few of them.

"Have you ever chewed bubble gum for about thirty seconds and then taken it out of your mouth? How does it feel? It's real sticky and yucky. Here in the middle of the floor is an imaginary circle. We've stayed up the past twenty-four hours and chewed piece after piece of bubble gum, each for thirty seconds. Then we have thrown it into our imaginary circle. Here in this circle are 9,997 pieces of slightly chewed bubble gum.

"Here we have a family. 'Miss, please come up! I want the rest of you to meet Tammy. She is thirty-five years old, a mother of three, a wonderful mom. She has a full time job. Just an incredible lady. Since she's been a young adult, Tammy has gone out each weekend to drink with her friends, but it doesn't seem to have been a problem. All of a sudden as Tammy is going through life, she steps right in the bubble gum. She's stuck. 'Try to move, Tammy.'

"Well, I'm trying, but I can't really move too much," says Tammy.

"That's right, you can't move too much. That's addiction. People get stuck. Watch Tammy. She can sway from side to side. She really thinks she's not stuck, that she can get out of that really quickly, but she can't.

"What happens as time goes on is that Tammy becomes more and more preoccupied with the gum while she's stuck in it. She isn't doing as good a job at work. She's out sick a lot. She isn't as productive because she's preoccupied with the gum. It's really starting to slow her down. She doesn't have freedom of choice anymore. When it comes to her kids, she can't take care of them like she used to. She's trapped in that gum. She's stuck! She's not spending as much time with her kids. She prepares dinner and just goes off on her own.

"Tammy has a husband named Fred. Fred loves his wife very much. Fred's been very concerned about Tammy. 'Haven't you, Fred?'

"Why, yes," says Fred.

"Fred has been concerned because he notices his wife is stuck in the gum. She's on probation at work because she has been absent so many days. Her last review wasn't very good. Fred has noticed over the past few months that he has had to take on more and more of the responsibilities at home. He's starting to prepare dinner. Fred is also spending time helping the kids with their homework and helping them with their projects on the weekend. He's very concerned about his wife. He doesn't get to spend as much time with her alone because she seems preoccupied and distant. She's just stuck in that gum.

"Because Fred cares for and loves his wife what do you suppose he tries to do? He tries to free his wife from the bubble gum. So go ahead, Fred, go and try to help your wife.

"As Fred tries to help his wife, he gets stuck in the bubble gum too. Try to move around, Fred. Notice, he thinks he can move around and he thinks he's free. But he's really stuck. Remember that addiction is a progressive disease. When Tammy first got stuck, the gum only went up to her calf. Now when Fred is stuck with her, it comes all the way up to their knees! How does this affect Fred? Now he's preoccupied at work. He's thinking about having to come home and prepare meals. He wonders if Tammy is going to be drunk or sober. Will she embarrass him at the family dinner next week? He thinks more and more about her. He's not available to his kids on a consistent basis anymore. He's not always helping them with their homework. Fred is even beginning to drink with Tammy sometimes. So all of a sudden he's stuck.

"We then have the oldest child, Jimmy. Jimmy's very concerned because not only is Mom stuck, but Dad's stuck too. Neither parent is there for him on a consistent basis. Out of love and concern, he tries to help them get unstuck. As Jimmy tries to get his parents unstuck look what happens. He also gets stuck in the gum. How does this affect Jimmy? His life isn't as free.

"How does this happen? Jimmy has a hard time concentrating in school. He thinks about having to go home to take care of a younger brother and sister. He's thinking about whether or not he should bring friends home. He might get embarrassed by what's happening there. Jimmy doesn't have very many opportunities to play anymore because he's taking care of his younger brother and sister. When he does have a chance to play, he's often worried about Mom and Dad. He might be yelled at for something he didn't do.

"As younger brother and sister attempt to help Mom, Dad, and Jimmy get unstuck from the bubble gum, they will get stuck too. The entire family gets stuck. That's the Bubble Gum Family. Why do the kids get stuck? This is important. Why do kids get stuck in the bubble gum? They get stuck because they try to help their parents first. So if kids get stuck because they try to help, how do kids get unstuck? Kids get unstuck when they stop trying to take care of other people in the family like Mom, Dad, brothers, or sisters. They can begin to take good care of themselves. That's how kids get unstuck from the bubble gum.

"What does it mean to take care of yourself? Go out and play. Talk to a teacher. Ask a counselor for help. Go to a neighbor's house. Call Grandma if there's a mess at the house and you don't want to be there. These are some different ways kids can take care of themselves.

"Notice how everyone attempted to help Tammy. They were all around her. Everyone got stuck in the bubble gum. Even if she wanted to get unstuck, she couldn't! There was no room for her to get out. The family had blocked her path to recovery. Kids need to take care of themselves and not get stuck caring for others first.

"We have to remember that recovery takes time. There might be a time when Jimmy starts to take good care of himself and gets unstuck, but two weeks from now there will be a big dinner at the house with Dad's business associates. Mom is still stuck in the bubble gum, so Jimmy might have to do a lot of the preparations.

"Recovery is a process. We take two steps forward, and because we're human, sometimes we take a step backward. So we get stuck and unstuck.

"That's the Bubble Gum Family."

This activity is adapted from *Kids' Power: Healing Games for Children of Alcoholics*.

Treatment-n-Recovery

(Ages six and up)

A logical extension of the Addiction Game, this visual and kinesthetic activity helps children gain a new and deeper understanding of the recovery process. They also come to see that they are not responsible for their parents' recovery, but that they are responsible for caring for themselves.

Description

In the Addiction Game, the dependent eventually gets hooked by the disease of addiction (role-played by the facilitator). The disease grabs the person by the arms and won't let him or her go, thus symbolizing how that person has been hooked, trapped, and consumed by addiction. After a brief discussion about how addiction now runs that individual's life, youngsters try different ways to get the person unstuck, all to no avail. Group members not only see that the addiction is not their fault, but also that they can't make everything better. This is the essence of the Addiction Game.

But how do people get better from addiction? While the disease still firmly has a grasp on the dependent, the group brainstorms ways in which the person can get better. When someone yells that the addicted person needs to ask for and get help, the dependent yells out, "Help. I need help. Please help." Role-playing Treatment-n-Recovery, the other facilitator makes his or her way to the person asking for help. When Treatment-n-Recovery gets close, the disease runs away out of fear. Treatment-n-Recovery introduces itself to the dependent and shares how it can help. "I'll help you learn to love yourself, be honest, share feelings, and learn how to take care of yourself and be free." The dependent learns that Treatment-n-Recovery only stays around if the person really wants to get better. Treatment-n-Recovery demonstrates that it is a safety net that protects the person from alcohol, other drugs, or whatever the person is hooked on. The disease lurks on the other side of the room, waiting to pounce on the dependent, but it can't do so while Treatment-n-Recovery is around.

All group members get the opportunity to role-play the dependent and ask Treatment-n-Recovery for help. A discussion follows on all the things that comprise Treatment-n-Recovery: treatment, continuing care, counseling, and 12-Step meetings like AA, NA, Al-Anon, etc.

Example

Julia yelled for help and was quickly met by Treatment-n-Recovery. At first, this six-year-old stood behind Treatment-n-Recovery for support and protection. With the disease lurking across the room and Julia feeling safer, she came out from behind Treatment-n-Recovery and started taunting the disease. "You'll never get me again, you big creep," she boasted amidst the giggles and laughter of the group. Growing braver by the second, Julia moved toward the disease as it whispered softly, "Come and say it right to me." Leaving Treatment-n-Recovery, Julia got close to the disease to utter those same words when she got hooked by it again. The facilitators briefly stopped the game and asked the group what had happened. Bertha yelled out, "She got hooked again. That's relapse. You leave Treatment-n-Recovery and you can have a relapse." What insight for this bright child!

Affirmations

- "It's okay to ask for help."
- "There are safe people and places to turn to for help."

Comments

- Emphasize that relapse also is not the child's fault. It occurs because the addicted person doesn't stay with Treatment-n-Recovery.
- During each child's role-play pick a different process or substance, such as alcohol, cocaine, pain medication, other drugs, food, work, exercise, gambling, or shopping for them to be hooked on. This adds depth and richness to the experience.
- If your group has only one facilitator, pick a child to play Treatment-n-Recovery.

Feelings

Stuffed Problems and Feelings
(Ages six and up)

This experiential exercise helps children to kinesthetically understand the consequences of holding problems and feelings inside. In a fun way, it also introduces them to the recovery process of identifying problems and expressing feelings. Youngsters actually experience freedom by initiating this process for themselves.

Description

With the children sitting in a circle, the group facilitator places a tote bag in the middle. Unbeknownst to the kids the bag is full of brightly colored rocks, each with a problem (such as addiction, fighting, abuse, and family secrets) or a feeling (such as anger, scared, hurt, shame, guilty, and sad) painted on it. The facilitator describes how everyone who comes to treatment has been carrying around such a bag inside. One by one, the kids pick up the bag and attempt to walk around the room carrying it. The facilitator asks such questions as, "How does it feel carrying all this stuff? When you carry such a heavy load what are you always thinking about? Can you be free to be a kid and laugh and play when you've always got that bag with you?"

After a brief discussion, the facilitator brings the bag to the middle of the circle and opens it up and explores its contents. One by one the children reach into the bag, take out a rock, and read the problem or feeling on it. When the addiction rock comes out the facilitator asks how many kids have addiction problems in their families. Many hands are raised. The facilitator acknowledges the children and states, "We'll learn lots about addiction, especially that it's not the kids' fault." When a feeling rock is pulled out the facilitator asks how many children have felt this way, and kids have a chance to share feelings. Before long the bag is empty and everyone has the chance to carry it around again. All are amazed at how much lighter the bag is because they talked about their problems and feelings.

Example

Jared, age six, could barely lift the full bag off the floor and had to drag it across the room. He especially enjoyed how much lighter it felt after the sharing session. At the end of the discussion he uttered, "I want to get rid of some rocks about Mom's divorce. I feel sad and scared."

Affirmations

- "I can share my problems and feelings with people who care."
- "All my feelings are okay."

Comments

- This is an excellent introductory activity to get the group rolling.
- As youngsters share problems and express feelings during the group, celebrate their progress by acknowledging "You let go of a couple more rocks today. Hooray!"

Materials

- Tote bag
- Twelve rocks, each painted with an individual feeling or problem

Guess My Feeling Game

(Ages six and up)

This fast-paced activity assists youngsters in identifying and expressing their feelings while developing congruency between their inner feelings and outer appearances.

Description

The facilitator begins the game by asking a volunteer to come forward and whisper a feeling in the facilitator's ear. The youngster then turns his or her back to the group. The facilitator directs the group to chant the magic chorus, "Turn, turn, turn in place, with a feeling on your face." As the group chants, the child slowly turns around and silently shows the feeling. After the expression is correctly identified, the child shares a time he or she experienced that particular feeling. The facilitator helps youngsters use "I" statements in sharing feelings.

This game works best when enough time is allotted to give each group member at least two chances to show a feeling to be guessed. The group facilitator follows up this exercise with a brief discussion about how we all have lots of similar feelings every day and that it's okay to talk about them with people we trust.

Example

Rachel was extremely shy on the first day and had not spoken more than a handful of words. With some gentle prodding from the facilitator she finally did the Guess My Feeling Game with some help from the others. When the group correctly guessed "Angry," Rachel whispered that she gets angry when Dad screams at her. Then she put her head down and quietly started to cry.

Affirmations

- "I can share my feelings if I feel safe."
- "My feelings belong to me."

Comments

- An option here is to have the children look in a mirror after they put their feeling faces on. This is a powerful way for kids to develop congruency on the outside for the feelings they experience on the inside.
- Assist shy children in doing this exercise by offering to do it with them. After they've tried it once, they are usually ready to go solo the next time.
- Sometimes it's necessary to give a child some assistance, not only in picking a feeling but also in creating the facial expression that can go along with it.

The Feelings Place

(Ages six and up)

This activity gets children moving as they explore their feelings. On their journey youngsters have the opportunity to identify and express a variety of emotions. They also learn that they can experience more than one feeling at a time.

Description

Strategically situated around the room are feeling regions, Lonely Land, Sad State, Angry Area, Happy Haven, Fear Forest, Shame Station, and Hurt Hideout. Each region is clearly marked with a poster stating its name, with a corresponding feeling face above it. The safari begins as the facilitator and the children roam the wilderness in search of feelings. As each feeling region is discovered the group stops and each person shares a time he or she felt that emotion. As the journey continues through each region, the facilitator acknowledges and validates every person's feelings and stresses that all feelings are okay and normal.

After all lands have been discovered, the group sits on the floor in the middle of the room. The facilitator puts a deck of index cards face down in the middle of the circle. The cards each feature a scenario for the youngsters to think about, such as being picked on by a school bully, parents fighting, having a big birthday party, or a parent drinking alcohol. The facilitator selects a child to choose an index card and read it to the group. After a few seconds the facilitator asks the children to go to the feeling region that represents how they would feel if this situation really happened to them. The youngsters scurry about the room until they find the appropriate region for themselves. The facilitator visits each land to ask the youngsters why they stopped there. The game continues until each child has had a chance to read a scenario from the index cards.

Example

No matter what scenario the index card described, Becka faithfully headed to Happy Haven. The other children were spread among the various feeling regions and often Becka was alone. At the end of the activity Becka shared that she always, always felt happy inside. The facilitator asked, "What about when Mom yells at you?" The smile quickly disappeared from Becka's face and her eyes filled with tears. With the support of her peers she walked ever so slowly to Fear Forest. The facilitator explained that it's okay to feel afraid sometimes; it's okay to feel lots of different feelings.

Affirmations

- "Feelings are my friends. I can listen to them."
- "I can have more than one feeling at a time."

Comments

- After each scenario is read the children may need enough time to visit more than one feeling region. The facilitator can explain that it's okay to have more than one feeling at a time.
- The facilitator may need to assist younger children in reading the scenario on the index card.

Materials

- Posters with feeling designations and matching feeling faces
- Index cards with various scenarios

Feeling Puppets

(Ages four and up)

Children of all ages particularly enjoy working with puppets, especially four- to six-year-olds. The puppets cast a magical spell on the children. They have little difficulty expressing anger, sadness, fear, and guilt through the puppets.

Description

Angry Amy, Sad Sam, Fearful Frankie, Guilty Gail, Happy Harry, and Confused Connie are the Feeling Puppet Family. (See examples in Figure 1.) They are sock puppets that children can easily manipulate. Each puppet has the initial of its respective feeling emblazoned on its tummy. The puppets live in an addicted family.

Using empty pop bottles to stand the puppets upright, they are placed in a semicircle. Each puppet has an identifying placard. This helps children remember their names. The group facilitators describe various problems between Mom and Dad puppets in two- to three-minute sequences: confrontations about drinking and using drugs, verbal abuse, threats of divorce, and family fighting. Children then pick the puppet that best represents how they would feel if they lived in the Feeling Puppet Family. They share the puppet's feelings and tell why they feel that way. Children may take turns to be more than one feeling puppet in the family.

Example

Here are some comments from eight-year-olds who recently played this game:

Confused Connie—"Why does Daddy still drink when he promised me he would stop? I don't understand."

Happy Harry—"I'm happy when Dad drinks because then I get away with murder."

Guilty Gail—"If I just could be a better kid, I know my parents would stop drinking."

Affirmations

- "All of your feelings are okay."
- "There are safe people you can talk to about your feelings."

Comments

- This is an extremely powerful activity to help children share feelings in the safety of communicating through puppets.
- Ideally, each child takes a turn with each puppet in order to share a number of feelings.

Materials

- Index card placards with the puppets' names
- Eight empty pop bottles
- Eight sock puppets

HAPPY HARRY   ANGRY AMY

Figure 1. Feeling Puppets

Feelings Box

(Ages six and up)

This game aids in the development of trust. It actively addresses feelings and problems by providing anonymity to those who cannot share openly because of trust issues. Children not only have fun playing this game, but they also have fun making it.

Description

A shoe box, old hat box, or cigar box can be used. Together, the children decorate the box by drawing or writing feelings on it, and pasting on feeling faces or words cut out from magazines. They can alternate between pasting, cutting, and drawing.

Then the children write or draw situations from their individual lives on colored index cards. They all place their card(s) in the box. In turn, each child picks a card, reads, or describes the situation, and talks about how the person may be feeling.

Example

Mackenzie, age nine, picked a card from the Feelings Box. She described a situation where Mom never came home in time to take the kids to the movie as she had promised. Mackenzie shared, "I feel sad and angry when my parents don't follow through with promises. It's just not fair." Other group members agreed with her and related similar experiences.

Affirmations

- "All your feelings are okay."
- "There are safe people I can talk to about my feelings."

Comments

- After each child's turn, you might want to open the discussion to more ideas and sharing.
- Sometimes children hesitate to share a feeling with the situation. Often this has to do with showing loyalty to Mom or Dad, or keeping the family secret.

Materials

- Adequate sized box
- Index cards
- Coloring materials
- Scissors
- Paste
- Magazines

Problem Solving and Self-Care

Wheel of Misfortune
(Ages six and up)

Children seem to love this game. It involves cooperation and teamwork in solving the real-life problems found in alcoholic and other drug-addicted families. Children come to see that they have choices and options in handling tough situations. It also prepares them to handle any similar real-life crisis in the future. While this is an activity children of all ages enjoy, the Wheel of Misfortune is particularly effective with six- to twelve-year-olds. Time flies when kids play this game.

Description

The facilitators divide children into groups of three, and each group selects a team name. With a spin of the wheel (see Figure 2) each team lands on a particular letter of the alphabet. The team looks at the Wheel of Misfortune gameboard to identify its problem, e.g., driving with a drunk parent or being embarrassed by a drinking parent in the presence of one's friends (see figure 3). The team brainstorms a variety of ways to solve the dilemma.

Facilitators emphasize the importance of taking good care of yourself and always staying safe. When all groups are ready, each team presents its findings to the large group. Discussion ensues.

Example

Evan, Jeremy, and Lori, all nine years old, called their team The Cool Cats. With a spin of the wheel they found Mom passed out on the living room rug. What to do? The suggestions flew back and forth—some silly, some outrageous, others ingenious. Evan suggested that they go get a neighbor. Lori wanted to call 911. Jeremy said, "It's a good idea to try and wake Mom first." They finally agreed to do all three—try to revive Mom, call 911 for an ambulance, and then get a neighbor. They were met with clapping when they shared with the larger group.

Affirmations

- "You can make helpful choices in your life."
- "It's good to take care of yourself."

Comments

- Play the game over and over to allow each team to brainstorm ways of handling a variety of problem situations. This helps them believe they truly have choices in their lives.

• Above all, this is an activity that stresses trust and cooperation among the children. The key here is teamwork. Everyone wins.

Materials

• Spinning Wheel
• Wheel of Misfortune gameboard

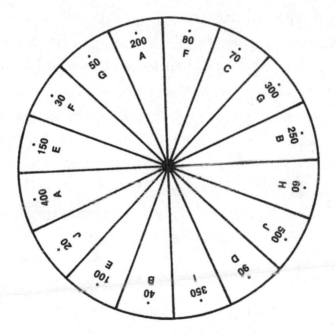

Figure 2. Wheel of Misfortune

A) Unsafe touch

B) Yelled at for no reason

C) Passed out on the floor

D) Driving with a drunk parent

E) Mom or Dad not coming home

F) Watching parent getting beat up

G) Brother or sister getting hit

H) Asked if you want alcohol or drugs

I) Embarrassed

J) Stuck in the middle

Figure 3. Wheel of Misfortune Gameboard

Jeopardy, the Self-Care Game

(Ages eight and up)

Combining the fun and excitement of a familiar television game show with learning basic self-care concepts, Jeopardy teaches youngsters a variety of ways to take good care of themselves. This game is played in a context of teamwork and cooperation where everyone wins.

Description

The facilitator divides the group into two teams and asks each one to select a group name. Once completed the facilitator introduces the five Jeopardy categories by writing them on newsprint or on a greaseboard in the front of the room. The categories for the self-care game are body, mind, feelings, spirit, and being a kid. The facilitator explains that these are the areas for kids to focus on when taking good care of themselves. Giving each team paper, pencils, and a clipboard to write on, the facilitator instructs them to brainstorm self-care ideas in each area. The facilitator moves between the groups and offers support, suggestions, and encouragement. Ten minutes usually suffices for this part of the activity.

Now both groups sit in front of the newsprint or greaseboard and the facilitator serves as the host. After everyone hums the *Jeopardy* theme song, the game begins. Starting with the body category, each team takes turns suggesting a self-care strategy for that topic. The facilitator writes each appropriate response under that category heading. The facilitator may also offer suggestions to assist the children in this process. The game continues until it weaves its way through the mind, feelings, spirit, and being a kid topics. The object of the game is to fill the newsprint or greaseboard with ideas for taking good care of oneself. A discussion follows in which the facilitator describes how youngsters may be in jeopardy if they fail to take the necessary time for self-care.

Example

Aubrey, usually very quiet during group, didn't seem very excited about playing Jeopardy. She started to get interested during the laughter and giggling as everyone hummed the theme song. With encouragement she participated in her team's discussion. Somehow she felt safer participating in the smaller group. With each suggestion she made, Aubrey's confidence grew. Aubrey contributed a variety of self-care ideas. "This is fun," she shared during the discussion. "I really do have lots of good ways to take care of myself." She beamed as a smile filled her face.

Affirmations

"It's important for me to take good care of myself."

"I deserve to take good care of myself."

"It's okay to ask for help. I don't have to do things all by myself."

Comments

• Follow up this game with Self-Care Bags. Having self-care ideas on the newsprint or greaseboard lends itself to this activity.

• Stress the importance of learning from one another in this game. The purpose of creating teams is to make the groups smaller and emotionally safer, yet the object is for the teams to collectively fill the board with good ideas.

Materials

- Newsprint or greaseboard
- Markers
- Paper
- Pencils
- Clipboards

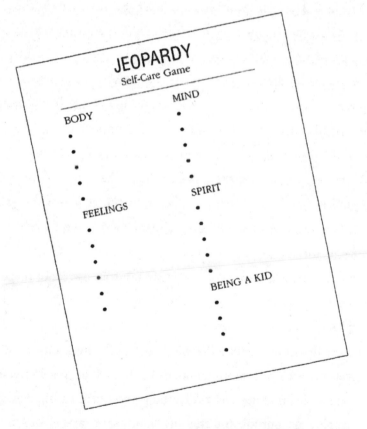

Example of Jeopardy: The Self-Care Game

Self-Care Bags

(Ages seven and up)

This exercise empowers children to incorporate self-care strategies into their daily lives. One of the few activities kids actually take home with them, self-care bags remind children of the importance to take time out for themselves because they deserve it.

Description

The facilitator distributes small lunch bags and instructs the children to decorate them. They may use crayons, colored pencils, and markers in any way they like, just as long as each child writes his or her name on the bag. Have plenty of extra bags available in case someone makes a mistake or ends up not liking his or her design. Kids usually need twenty minutes or so to complete the activity, but the facilitator should give the group extra time, if necessary.

After the bags are finished, the facilitator hands each youngster five index cards. Using the results from the Jeopardy Self-Care Game on the newsprint or greaseboard (see Jeopardy Self-Care Game in this section), the facilitator asks the children to write down a self-care idea on each side of the five index cards. Youngsters have visual cues in the areas of body, mind, feelings, spirit, and being a kid from the Jeopardy game to use as ideas to write on the index cards. The facilitator tells the group to write suggestions for each of the areas listed above so that youngsters will be sure to include ideas for taking good care of their bodies, minds, feelings, spirits, and the little kid inside each of them.

After the children have completed this phase, the facilitator instructs them to put their completed index cards into their care bags. Sitting in a circle, the children, one by one, take out a card and read each side for self-care ideas. The facilitator explains the importance of having a suggestion on each side, as children have choices in how they can take care of themselves.

A discussion ensues about the importance of caring for oneself. The facilitator brainstorms with the group ways they can use their bags when they get home: "If you're ever bored or not feeling very good about yourself, pull a card out of the bag and follow the instructions; use your self-care bag on a daily basis."

Example

Tamika looked very sad after getting into an argument with another group member during break. As she acknowledged her sadness to the facilitator, she took his suggestion of pulling a card out of her self-care bag. She didn't like the suggestion on one side, "Play a game." On the other side it said, "Tell someone your feelings." After a few moments of contemplation Tamika told the group, "I feel sad when people call me names." A rich discussion followed as this ten-year-old really did take care of herself.

Affirmations

"I can take good care of myself."

"I deserve to take good care of myself."

"I can make good choices to take care of me"

Comments

- This activity works very well as a follow-up to Jeopardy, the Self-Care Game.
- Use the self-care bags throughout the program to help the group practice using them to take care of themselves.

Materials

- Small lunch bags
- Crayons, markers, colored pencils
- Index cards

Safe People Maps

(Ages seven and up)

This activity assists kids in deepening their awareness of what makes certain people safe and others not so safe. By consciously searching for characteristics of safe people, children soon have maps to determine whom they can turn to in times of need.

Description

During one of the initial group sessions, the facilitator introduces the concept of safe people. Children discuss whom they turn to when they need support and guidance. More important, they begin to ponder what it is that makes that person safe. Taking a large piece of newsprint with "Safe People" written on the top and taping it to the wall during each session, the facilitator guides a brief discussion about characteristics that help make someone safe. At first, even six-year-olds share two things about safe people: they don't laugh at you when you ask for help, and they don't blab what you tell them to just about everyone.

By taking five minutes near the end of each group, children can add new data based on the concepts and learning that have taken place during that session. Before long this exercise becomes spontaneous as kids yell out new characteristics as soon as they come to mind. For example, Robbie contributed the idea that safe people aren't always drinking or using other drugs. Lucy added that safe people often share their feelings with others, including her.

Toward the end of the program, the list contains numerous

characteristics. The facilitator takes ample time during one of the last groups to have the children brainstorm who in their lives has many of these gifts and skills (probably no one has them all, because no one's perfect). The facilitator provides extra support for those who have trouble translating the list into people in their lives. Finally, everyone gets a copy of the list (Safe People Map) and is encouraged to add to it as they go through life.

Example

At the end of a group devoted to feelings, Barry quickly raised his hand when it came time to discuss new characteristics for safe people. This twelve-year-old floored the group facilitators with this astute observation: "Safe people listen with their eyes. They really show they care." Barry greatly added to the richness of the list and certainly gave the facilitators something to think about.

Affirmations

- "I can learn about safe people."
- "There are safe people I can turn to for help."

Comments

- The facilitator may guide the process by helping youngsters touch upon any important points that escape them about safe people.

Materials

- A sheet of newsprint with "Safe People" written on it
- Masking tape

- Markers
- Safe People Maps

Example of a Safe People Map

Alphabet Soup
(Ages seven and up)

This activity goes beyond helping kids understand that addiction is not their fault. While this game helps children know in their hearts they are not responsible for their parents' problems, it also guides them in learning how they can take good care of themselves. Youngsters come to realize that self-care is ultimately their most important responsibility.

Description

The facilitator distributes the updated Alphabet Soup sheets (see example at the end of this activity) to group members. One by one youngsters volunteer to read one of the Seven Cs. The children briefly discuss the meaning of each C and share how it applies to their lives before moving on to the next C. The facilitator then explains that the Seven Cs can actually be divided into two parts: things you are not responsible for (the first three Cs) and things you are (the final four Cs). A discussion follows in which the group differentiates between these two categories. The facilitator reiterates that children can't make their parents' problems better, but they can learn to take care of themselves.

Children can either color their Alphabet Soup sheet with crayons and markers or draw a picture on the back of the sheet. The pictures can either illustrate how family addiction really isn't the children's fault or show a new way children can take good care of themselves. Another option, if time permits, is to divide the

Seven Cs among group members and have them make collages illustrating the message of each C. Youngsters paste the pictures and words they cut out of magazines onto large poster boards. During group discussion, children look at the various collages and guess which C each one represents.

Example

Frankie had difficulty playing Alphabet Soup. He told the group facilitator that he was very angry he had to do a collage about CELEBRATE me. "It's not fair. Why can't I do one on can't CONTROL or can't CURE?" he bluntly asked the facilitator. Not getting the response he wanted, Frankie sat in a corner and stared off into space. After a few minutes had passed, the facilitator approached Frankie and validated his anger. "It's real hard for you to let go of Mom's problems and just focus on yourself," the facilitator gently offered. Tears quickly welled up in Frankie's eyes as he nodded affirmatively. Even though he never completed the collage, he clearly got the point of this exercise.

Affirmations

- "It's important to take good care of myself."
- "I can let go of my parents' problems."
- "I'm learning about what I'm responsible for and what I'm not."

Comments

- Whether children draw pictures or make collages, hang the artwork on the walls during subsequent sessions. It will serve as a powerful visual reminder of exactly what youngsters can and can't do in their daily lives.

It's often necessary, particularly with younger children, for the facilitator to provide extra assistance and support as the group members work on their drawings and/or collages. Simply roaming around the room and checking in with each child can make a big difference.

Materials

- Alphabet Soup sheets
- Crayons and markers
- Poster board
- Magazines
- Scissors
- Glue

(The last four items are for the collage option.)

It's important for kids from addicted families to remember the 7 Cs.

The 7 Cs:

- I didn't CAUSE it.
- I can't CONTROL it.
- I can't CURE it.
- But I can learn to take CARE of myself

by—

- COMMUNICATING feelings.
- Making healthy CHOICES and
- CELEBRATING myself.

Self-Worth

Living Cards

(Ages eight and up)

This powerful exercise in peer affirmation is incredibly helpful in promoting self-esteem. If at all possible, do this exercise on the floor. Kids get more out of Living Cards if they sprawl across the room. Play some of their favorite music softly in the background.

Description

Have the children find places on the floor with plenty of room. Give each of them a piece of white paper (8½" x 11"). Spread crayons, colored markers, and pencils across the floor. Ask each child to write his or her name in the middle of the page. Encourage the children to be creative with different colors and specialized lettering (e.g., block or script). Then ask them to reflect silently on the special qualities everyone contributes to the group. No one does any writing yet. (Because the kids have been with one another in group this shouldn't be difficult.) The facilitators can provide a few examples to help people get started.

After a few minutes, the children pass their papers to the left, and their neighbors write briefly about the special qualities of the person whose name is on the sheet. This continues until each paper has gone around the group and come back to the owner. Take time for each group member to absorb the special things that have been written about him or her. Then everyone has a chance to share his or her Living Card with the others. Ask how each child feels about the comments on his or her card. Children may take their Living Cards home. Many hang them in their rooms; others have them framed (see sample card at the end of this activity).

Example

Ten-year-old Steven was having a rough time. He believed he couldn't do anything right and didn't fit in. He wanted to go home. During the Living Cards exercise, others wrote about his courage, swimming ability, and friendliness. When Steven read his card, he lit up like a Christmas tree. He came to see himself in a new way. His eyes filled with tears when he told the group, "Thanks, I guess I really am okay."

Affirmations

- "Everyone has special qualities."
- "I am a beautiful and special person."

- "It's okay to feel good about myself."

Comments

- This activity works with younger kids if the facilitators write for them. A variation on this theme is to have the little ones draw a picture of what's special about the others, such as a flower, the sunshine, a rainbow, or a favorite toy.

Despite concern that group members might write derogatory comments about one another, we have rarely seen this happen. The facilitators must set the tone for this exercise by sharing, and they must also participate with their own cards.

Materials

- White paper
- Crayons
- Colored pencils or markers
- Tablets of paper

Example of Living Card

This activity is taken from *Kids' Power: Healing Games for Children of Alcoholics*

I Am Special Bags

(Ages six and up)

This simple activity helps youngsters discover the buried treasure they possess inside. Children especially enjoy reflecting to
group members their specialness while basking in the warm reflec-
tions sent by the others.

Description

The facilitator passes out lunch bags and decorating materials to
the group and instructs the children to decorate their bags and put
their first names on them. The facilitator allows fifteen minutes or
more for this activity. Have extra bags available in case youngsters
make a mistake or don't like their final creations. After the children
are finished, the facilitator collects the bags and lines them up at
the front of the room. Each child is then given several blank index
cards, and the facilitator instructs the group to write a special
quality of each group member on a separate card and then drop it
into that person's bag.

Once everyone's bag is full, the facilitator gives the group a few
minutes to read their cards. The facilitator asks each child to share
a compliment or two from his or her bag. A discussion follows
about how everyone has special qualities and that it's okay to feel
good about yourself. Then the children write the words "I am special" on their bags. They may take their bags with them as a
reminder of all their special qualities.

Example

Rosa, a quiet and shy seven-year-old, methodically checked the contents of her bag. Surprisingly, she wanted to share two of her gifts with the group. Rosa uttered very softly, "Smart and kind." A thin smile appeared on her face as the others clapped and cheered for her. It was the first time she had ever really smiled in group.

Affirmations

- "I can celebrate my special qualities."
- "It's okay to feel good about myself."

Comments

- Have younger children draw something special about each person in group. Employ this strategy as well for youngsters who have difficulty with reading and writing activities.
- Make sure that each member does a card for every other person in group. Help youngsters to realize the importance of this activity by making sure the facilitators decorate a bag and fully participate as well.

Materials

- Lunch bags
- Decorating materials (markers, crayons, construction paper, scissors, and glue)
- Blank index cards

My Great Plate

(Ages eight and up)

A spin-off on Living Cards, this lively activity gets youngsters up and moving as they communicate special qualities to one another.

Description

The facilitator spreads crayons, colored pencils, and markers across the floor, then hands a white piece of cardboard to each group member. As in Living Cards, the facilitator instructs the kids to creatively write their first name in the middle of the cardboard. It is helpful to provide a few finished products as examples (script letters, bubble letters, different colors) to spark group members' creativity.

After the youngsters have completed their masterpieces, the facilitator punches two holes at the top of each piece of cardboard, then gives the children yarn to put through the holes and instructs them to tie a knot so that the Great Plate can be worn around their necks. The facilitator provides assistance to children who need help tying their knots.

Wearing the plates around their necks, the kids brainstorm a variety of special qualities, which the facilitator records on newsprint or greaseboard for all to see. This list provides the group with visual cues to assist them in completing the task in a meaningful way. After putting their placards on their backs and out of view, the children walk around the room with a marker and write a special quality on each person's plate. Often a long train develops as Jimmy writes on Lisa's plate and Shelly writes on Jimmy's plate and Manuel writes on Shelly's plate. Once completed, the train needs to shift positions and continue with other plates. The shifting often produces lots of giggling and laughter. Once everyone has written on each plate the group sits in a circle on the floor. With two minutes of quiet time to find the "buried treasure," the children turn their plates around and read about their own special qualities. Everyone has a chance to share a few items from their plates, and a brief discussion follows on accepting compliments.

Example

Michael's Great Plate had really captivated him. As he scanned the many gifts others attributed to him, his eyes got wider and his smile broader. "I really get to take this home?" the eight-year-old asked. He giggled spontaneously when the group members nodded their heads.

Affirmations

- "It's okay to feel good about myself."
- "I can celebrate my special qualities."
- "I am a special and talented kid."

Comments

- This activity can work with younger children if they draw pictures to represent one another's qualities.
- It's important for the facilitator to participate in this activity with the children.

Materials

- White cardboard
- Hole punch
- Yarn
- Markers, crayons, colored pencils
- Newsprint or greaseboard

Letter Special
(Ages seven and up)

A fun and affirming exercise, Letter Special assists youngsters in realizing their special qualities. Group members get valuable practice in giving and receiving compliments. Most of all, this activity gives children permission to celebrate their unique gifts.

Description

With the children spread out comfortably on the floor, the facilitator distributes paper and clipboards, then instructs youngsters to write their first names down the side of the paper with crayons, colored pencils, or markers. Group members may do so as creatively as possible, using special lettering (such as script, bubbled, or block) and different design and color combinations. The facilitator has extra paper on hand in case participants make a mistake or simply want to try something different. After everyone has finished, the facilitator collects the papers.

A brief discussion about special qualities follows as the group brainstorms a list of these traits, such as caring, honest, brave, smart, friendly, artistic, and gentle. The facilitator writes the group's thoughts on a greaseboard or newsprint. This valuable visual tool deeply enhances the quality of this experience.

Next the facilitator pulls out one paper from the pile and reads the name. Taking a moment to explain how people's names actually reflect some of their special gifts, the facilitator leads the group in brainstorming how each letter of the person's name represents one of his or her special gifts. For example, using Ben's name, the group came up with bright, energetic, and nice. After Ben agreed to these gifts, the facilitator wrote each one horizontally on the page (see example). The process continues until each person's paper is filled with some of their special qualities. The activity concludes with a long and loud group cheer.

The group was hard at work when it came to Phil's turn. Within moments the qualities proud, happy, intelligent, and loving were suggested. Phil accepted them all except proud, because he just didn't think it fit. For the next few minutes the group brainstormed to no avail, because Phil didn't think popular fit either. Finally the facilitator told Phil that it would be his task in the days ahead to find the right fit for P. Then the group celebrated the three qualities Phil had agreed upon. His smile almost filled the room.

Affirmations

- "Everyone has special qualities, including me."
- "It's okay to feel good about myself."
- "Today I will celebrate me."

Comments

- Take the time to brainstorm special qualities on the board.
- The facilitator can play an active role in the brainstorming process by giving the group lots of solid ideas.
- It is perfectly okay not to find a quality that fits every single letter in every person's name. Celebrate the letters of the person's name that you do come up with special gifts for, and let

the child keep searching for gifts that correspond to the letters that remain.

Materials

- Paper
- Clipboards
- Crayons
- Colored pencils
- Markers
- Greaseboard or newsprint

Example of Letter Special

Inside Special

(Ages seven and up)

This fun exercise reminds youngsters that their most special gifts are inside. It also deepens children's ability to give and receive affirmations.

Description

Prior to group, the facilitator writes two simple yet different affirmations on small strips of paper for every member in group, folds the strips in half, and puts them inside uninflated balloons. Inside Special works well as a final follow-up exercise to Living Cards or I Am Special Bags. After one of the above activities, the facilitator hands each child a balloon to blow up. Some youngsters may require assistance in inflating and tying their balloons.

After a brief follow-up discussion on celebrating special gifts, the facilitator instructs the children to pop their balloons with the pins provided and to explore the treasure within. Youngsters silently open the two affirmations and carefully read them. The facilitator then asks the members to put the affirmation that most suits them into their pockets and to give the other one to another person in the group. As youngsters give away the extra affirmation they get one in return from the person who received their affirmation. This process of giving and receiving may take up to three turns, at which point everyone keeps the affirmation in his or her possession. Children may share their affirmations with the group as the facilitator reviews how affirmations can help youngsters take good care of themselves.

Example

After all the giving and receiving had taken place, a sly grin appeared on Joanne's face. When asked about her affirmations, this ten-year-old proudly declared, "I am capable" and "I am a beautiful child of God." When asked if those affirmations fit her she quickly responded, "Oh, yes!" and the grin turned into a huge smile.

Affirmations

- "I am lovable and capable."
- "It's okay to feel good about myself."
- "I can celebrate my special qualities."

Comments

- Be prepared to assist youngsters who have difficulty reading. Keeping the written affirmations basic and simple is helpful in this regard. The facilitator participates in this activity by positively modeling how to give and receive compliments in a healthy, balanced way.

Materials

- Strips of paper with individual affirmations
- Balloons
- Pins

Bibliography

Abbott, S., ed. *Children of Alcoholics: Selected Readings.* NACoA, 1996.

———. *Children of Alcoholics: Selected Readings.* Vol. 2. NACoA, 2000.

Ackerman, R. J. *Children of Alcoholics: A Guidebook for Educators, Therapists, and Parents.* 2nd ed. Simon & Schuster, 1987.

———. *Perfect Daughters.* Rev. ed. Health Communications, Inc., 2002.

———. *Same House, Different Home.* Health Communications, Inc., 1987.

———. *Silent Sons.* Fireside, 1994.

Ackerman, R. J., P. Vegso, T. Peluso, and J. Canfield. *Chicken Soup for the Recovering Soul.* Health Communications, 2004.

Black, C. *It Will Never Happen to Me.* Hazelden, 2002.

———. *My Dad Loves Me, My Dad Has a Disease: A Child's View of Living with Addiction.* MAC Publishing, 1997.

Brown, S., and V. Lewis. *The Alcoholic Family in Recovery: A Developmental Model.* Guilford Press, 2002.

Brown, S., V. Lewis, and A. Liotta. *The Family Recovery Guide: A Map for Healthy Growth.* New Harbinger Publications, 2000.

Cork, R. M. *The Forgotten Children.* Paperjacks, 1969.

Deutsch, C. *Broken Bottles, Broken Dreams: Understanding and Helping Children of Alcoholics.* Teacher's College Press, 1982.

Moe, J. *The Children's Place . . . At the Heart of Recovery.* QuinnEssentials Books, 2003.

———. *Discovery . . . Finding the Buried Treasure: A Prevention/Intervention Program for Youth from High-Stress Families.* ImaginWorks, 1993.

Moe, J., C. Brown, and B. LaPorte. *Kids' Power Too: Words to Grow By.* ImaginWorks, 1996.

Moe, J., and T. Drennon. *The Beamer Series for Kids.* Betty Ford Center Publications, 2006–2007.

Moe. J., and D. Pohlman. *Kids' Power: Healing Games for Children of Alcoholics.* Health Communications, Inc., 1989.

Moe, J., and P. Ways. *Conducting Support Groups for Elementary Students K-6: A Guide for Educators and Other Professionals.* Johnson Institute, 1991.

Seixas, J., and G. Youcha. *Children of Alcoholics: A Survival Manual.* Harper and Row, 1985.

Wegscheider-Cruse, S. *Another Chance: Hope and Health for the Alcoholic Family.* Science and Behavior Books, 1981.

Werner, E., and R. Smith. *Journey from Childhood to Midlife: Risk, Resiliency and Recovery.* Cornell University Press, 2001.

Index